Praise for My Little Blue Branch

"In *My Little Blue Branch*, Susan Perry Benson does for her family ranch in Central Texas what John Graves did for the Brazos River in his landmark book *Goodbye to a River*: celebrates nature (and human nature) with a graceful, exact, and unsentimental eye. Also? It's really funny."

—MICHAEL PARKER, AUTHOR OF I AM THE LIGHT OF THIS WORLD AND 2022 INDUCTEE TO THE TEXAS INSTITUTE OF LETTERS,

MY LITTLE
Blue Branch
A TEXAS MEMOIR

SUSAN PERRY BENSON

The events and conversations in this book have been set down to the best of the author's ability, although some names and details have been changed to protect the privacy of individuals.
Photography is provided with permission by the author and her family except where noted.

First Printing, 2023

ISBN 979-8-9868814-0-9
1. Memoir 2. Personal Essay 3. Culture

Cover design: Cyn Macgregor
Interior layout: CynergieStudio.com
Editor: Suzanne Wood

Benson Tropical Press
7643 NC 50 North
Benson, NC 27504
www.susanperrybenson.com

Printed in the United States of America

My Little Blue Branch
A Texas Memoir

Susan Perry Benson

Dedication

To the loving memory of my parents,
Ivan and Josephine
And my grandparents,
Ivan and Elsie
And to all the children and descendants of
The Perry family
I dedicate this book.

Acknowledgments

Many hands went into the making of this book. And I have many to thank. I'd be remiss if I didn't include two people from the early days, both friends and mentors who paved my path to publication. Kinky Friedman, a Texas author, humorist, and songwriter, once said that an editor's job is to take a great book and make it good. The late Van Hetherly, my editor at *Texas*, the Sunday magazine section of the *Houston Chronicle*, would have loved the humor in that statement. He was responsible for egging me on as he patiently read my copy and published a piece now and then. With the passing of time, his mantras still echo through my mind: "Keep writing" or "The only person who can do the book is the person writing the check," in this case, me.

The Prologue (previously "Blue Hole, a Timeless Touchstone") and "The Sue-Ben" (previously "Life Floats Without a Boat") appeared in *Texas* in somewhat different forms after Van retired and Ken Hammond took the helm. Although Ken declined my first submission, an essay about the changes taking place in my old Houston neighborhood, he sent me a nice hand-written note that stated he wasn't looking for nostalgia. His note gave me permission to write it the way I'd intended, and my revised essay appeared in *Texas*. "Aunt Edna and the Road Less Traveled" was the last essay I sent him and appears within these pages. Ken loved it, but as many newspapers were downsizing, he couldn't get it into the magazine before it folded. We were both deflated about it, but such is a writer's life. He retired in 2004 and passed away in January of 2022 after teaching English and tutoring at Houston Community College for eighteen years.

First and foremost, I want to thank my editor and friend, Suzanne Wood, for fixing my misplaced modifiers, dangling participles, and "drop quotes." After reading my manuscript for the first time, she gave me the green light to carry on and take the plunge. I will be forever grateful for her encouragement and suggestions along the way.

A big shout out to my graphic artist, Cyn Macgregor, for holding my hand throughout the tedious process of cover design and formatting, two mountains I had to climb whether I liked it or not, and a big learning curve for me.

Thanks go to Lisa Rosen, author of *Indigo House*, for steering me in the right direction on indie publishing with suggested reading material, blogs and podcasts.

I want to extend a long arm of thanks to the Texas poets who gave me their permission to use excerpts from their poems: David E. Cowen, Stephanie Madan, and Margaret Dornaus.

My hand also goes out to Shelby Stephenson, Poet Laureate of North Carolina, for his fine poems.

Thanks to the nice ladies at the Heritage Center in La Grange, Texas, for locating and loading reels of microfilm from previous decades of the *La Grange Journal* and tirelessly looking up old census records.

I'll always feel indebted to my book club, a tightknit group of close friends who have read my essays and stories for the past twenty years: Sarah Smith, Donna Tolar, Danise Emory, Stephanye Sanderson, Ann Stephenson, Ann Benson, and the late Margaret Maron, who was both friend and mentor.

Thanks to my early beta readers: my brother Ben, Cathy Perry, Lauran English, Pam Perry, Fritzeen Scott, and Kay Burkhalter. Always good to get the feedback. And hats off to my nephew, Taylor and my niece Anne Aydinian Perry, for taking the time to proofread the galley print.

Thanks to my husband, Dan, and son, Kerry, who feed my spirit on a daily basis and support my art unflinchingly.

Prelude

Beneath the crisscrossed shadows of live oaks and a network of mustang grape vines, a small tributary of the Colorado River shimmers across gravel beds, riffles through a broken dam, whirling into a micro-eddy of feeding perch. Thumping and tumbling across forgotten stepping stones, its unbroken rhythm foams madly against a downed tree and escapes, traversing limestone ledges and resuming a mindless course. Sweeping past tufts of maidenhair fern, the crystal water carves geodesic lines in the landscape, spilling over a mossy green staircase into gin-clear pools below.

Stands of leafless candelilla, once prized by the Mexicans for making soap and candle wax, choke a narrow passage and give snug harbor to a cottonmouth water moccasin wallowing in the shallows. While leafcutter ants float on tiny leaf-boats, catching the current to the other side, frigid basins offer a drink to a passing spike buck or a bloated cow thirsty on clover.

Civil War survivors soaked their aching feet in the shallows and countless drifters have slept by a mesquite fire on its banks. Before White encroachment, legend has it that women of the Tonkawa Nation lay in the healing waters after childbirth. An occasional flood unearths enough flint spear points and arrowheads to fill a shoe box.

Gently threading the eye of a natural bridge, the creek cascades with tinkling dulcimer sounds into a large swimming hole, ever seeking its lowest point. The circular green pool mirrors weathered initials carved into lichen-covered boulders a century ago. The elements of time have altered this speck of Texas very little. A raccoon foraging along the bank has unknowingly gathered a coat full of preacher's lice, sticky green seeds he'll spread along the ancient trail of the Blue Branch.

Prologue

Texas has never been known for its trees, so whenever I'm giving newcomers directions to the Fayette County ranch that has been in our family for generations, I'll tell them to look for the giant live oak at the end of our gravel drive, a Heritage Oak according to a state arborist, and a landmark easily spotted from the highway. Dwarfing the house at seventy feet, it makes all the other trees in the county look like saplings, and has stood sentry for at least 500 years, maybe a thousand. If friends are running late, I'll stand under the oak and watch the blitz of traffic on the Austin Bypass, imagining a slower time, a time when my grandparents and great-grandparents traveled here in horse-drawn buggies along a dirt road that is now Texas 71. On hot summer days, locals used to file in and meet up for a refreshing dip in the swimming hole, and a well-worn footpath from the Perry Oak will take you there.

Our ranch is named after the Blue Branch, a quarter-mile, spring-fed creek that begins its short life in one corner of the ranch and ends at the "blue hole." It's obvious from hundreds of weathered initials carved into the surrounding sandstone boulders that this was once a hub of activity. Visitors familiar with the soft nature of sandstone dug in deep, and those initials are the most distinct today. The day my grandparents carved their initials into a slab upstream, they, too, were visitors—teenage newlyweds with a dream, eloping with only the clothes on their backs and Granddad's promise to buy his bride a new dress. Recalling their early years together, Grandfather would say, "We were poor as church mice," and Grandmother would chuckle, "We weren't poor, we just didn't have any *money*."

After a few good years farming cotton with their three boys on the other side of La Grange, they fulfilled a decade-long dream and bought the Blue Branch from the F.J. Mohrhusen family. They tore down the old homestead my grandfather had lived in as a boy, utilizing some of the lumber to build the arts and crafts bungalow that sits there today. They struggled through the Depression years, eating rooster chili and selling outlying parcels of the ranch to survive, one famous, or infamous parcel being the land that later housed the Chicken Ranch, aka the *Best Little Whorehouse in Texas*. Despite their hardships, they managed to keep the heart and soul of the place: the blue hole.

Prior to World War II, the blue hole took on all the elements of a public park. It wasn't unusual to have ten or fifteen cars parked nearby while families and scout troops enjoyed picnics and churches held baptisms—usually unannounced, but welcome just the same. My father and his friends formed a swim club and built two bathhouses from scrap lumber. But after the war, a new public pool in town became the big draw and locals deserted the blue hole, those weathered initials the graffiti of a bygone era. After Granddad retired from the railroad (he'd been a fireman with Southern Pacific), my grandparents relocated to Houston and rented out the ranch house. Sometime in the 1950s, during their absence, the railroad replaced the trestle that spanned the confluence of the Blue Branch and Cedar Creek with two large culverts just below the swimming hole. A hike to the blue hole being priority one, my grandfather made this shocking discovery during one of his weekly trips to check on his cattle. Nothing pleased him more than gazing at a slick, healthy cow, but the Blue Branch was about as sacred to him as the Rock of Ages. He was appalled to find that his cows refused to walk through the irregular cylinders for water in Cedar Creek at the other end.

An attorney advised him that the previous landowners had sold the right-of-way to the railroad with the understanding there would be no obstruction that might hinder cattle. After a round of letters, the railroad paved the base of these "tunnels" with asphalt, but to no avail. Floods washed away this blacktop Band-Aid and, over time, the blue hole started to shrink from a backwash of gravel and logjams. Despite Grandad's many complaints, the statute of limitations finally ran out, and the culverts remain to this day.

"Never underestimate the power of the railroad," he'd lament—one of the few times in his long life I ever saw him red-faced.

Though time and outside forces have taken a toll—the "hole" is about half its size and more of a semi-circle now—the water sliding over the fall still makes its own familiar music, and maidenhair ferns cling to the rocks at the waterline like an apron of green lace. Few outsiders know of our little oasis anymore, and finding the occasional arrowhead reminds me that we're only temporary caretakers here.

In the wintertime, I seek out the bluebonnet sprouts growing along the creek and predict the coming season—something I learned at Grandfather's knee. At all times it's a peaceful place to reflect or make a wish or not think at all, tucked away and invisible to all but the passing railroad engineer or the random deer stopping to drink. Six generations of my family have gathered strength here, the warp and woof of our lives so tightly woven nothing could tear it asunder. Much of my oral history has taken place on these rocks, family gatherings a predictable sequence of events. Within nanoseconds of parking in the shade of the Perry Oak, after hugs all around, my elders are off on a pilgrimage to the blue hole where they'll relive days of skinny-dipping in the dead of winter or Uncle Elo's bootlegging escapades during the Prohibition years or laugh about the time my feisty great-grandmother, a dyed-in-the-wool Southern Baptist, tipped over the crocks of mustang grape wine fermenting in the barn.

Sooner or later the spirits of my grandparents catch up with me here, and I feel their presence all the more at Christmas. In one memory, Grandfather has just spiked the eggnog, the most risqué thing I ever saw him do. "Don't touch those bubble lights, they'll burn your little fingers," he warns. Santa's arrival is imminent, and because of his shy nature, we seven grandkids are herded outside where the adults congregate on the porch. Dizzy with excitement, I join my three girl cousins in the front yard to sing carols. Tomboys to the core, we're all dressed up in elegant taffeta gowns Grandmother worked on throughout the summer. After a few angelic rounds of "Silent Night," we hoist our frilly skirts and race across the lawn, jumping over the hedge like a pack of wild ponies. I can hear Grandmother giggling hysterically above all the laughter.

She spent her last Christmas in a Houston nursing home while I worked all morning trying to duplicate her recipes for cornbread stuffing and divinity, chopping and dicing and making a big mess. The divinity was a flop, but I took her a plate of the cornbread stuffing she'd asked for, her smile of approval between bites the best gift I got that year. When she died, I lost my best friend. After Grandfather's death ten months later, I felt like the great oak had fallen. They'd been together sixty-nine years. And I do mean together.

On any given pilgrimage to the blue hole, my thoughts will scatter. I might see Uncle Elo hightailing it through the briars, the revenuers in hot pursuit. Sometimes I'll hear the little-boy shrieks of my son and nephews as they plunge from a rope-swing into the blue-green water. I might see our last old horse, Sugar, stumbling blindly over the steep rim, neck-deep in the water for hours until my brother found her and the local vet hauled her to safety. But in my mind's eye, I will always see my elderly grandfather down on all fours. Dressed in his Sunday suit, pocketknife in hand, he's tracing over the initials he and his young bride carved into that sandstone slab on their wedding day: I. P. + E. S. —May 6, 1916. 🌿

Elsie and Ivan Perry with their sons, left to right, Lelldon, Fred and Ivan, 1929

Contents

Chapter 1 – Evolution Of A Cabin

Cicada wings, small
Yet surprisingly sturdy and resilient
May be found near pools of water
Perhaps below far-reaching limbs…
Though not the wings of fairies
As some children are told, it's possible
They trill tales of worlds beyond
The heated walls of this stifling afternoon

— TEXAS POETRY CALENDAR 2015 BY LAURAN PERRY ENGLISH

In the mid-1950s, living large to my family meant escaping city life and roughing it in a one-room cabin at the Blue Branch. Though only a two-hour drive from our place in Houston, the ranch seemed worlds away and felt more like the *real* Texas to me. The Blue Branch is situated in an area I like to call the foothills of the Texas Hill County, where prickly pear cactus, cedars and live oaks are the norm, and limestone bluffs jut out majestically over the Colorado River.

During the first leg of our trip from Houston to the town of Columbus, the scenery is rife with prairies and rice fields that spread like a Parcheesi board to the far horizon. After we'd exhausted our supply of comic books and sung a chorus or two of "The Eyes of Texas," "Oh Beautiful Texas," or "The Yellow Rose of Texas," Dad would stop and let us cool our jets at the Pie Place outside of Sealy. I don't know if that was the actual name, but that's what we called it because they sold every kind of pie known to man, by the slice or to carry.

The scenery changes dramatically west of Columbus, and after crossing the steel suspension bridge over the Colorado River, we'd perk up like rabid fruit bats, hanging over the front seat of our Plymouth sedan for a better view as the countryside begins to buck and roll and the bluffs rise up like long fossilized arms covered in green scrub.

Riding on the two-lane blacktop made every ranch we passed feel up close and personal; herds of grazing cattle, signs advertising Longhorns, Brahmans and Hereford steer, a cowhand checking fence-lines on horseback, the occasional pump jack nodding in the distance. If we begged long and hard enough, Dad sometimes made a quick stop at the "Hanging Tree" outside of Columbus. He was a teenager in 1935 when a mob wearing masks overpowered the local sheriff and lynched two teenaged black boys accused of raping and killing a young White woman. Allegedly, they'd confessed to the crime and were about to stand trial. Looking back through the eyes of an adult, I will always wonder about their guilt or innocence, leaning heavily toward their innocence. A pink granite historical marker was placed there in 1936 noting the centennial of Colorado County, not the hanging.

Hank's Place was another landmark on the highway just up the hill from the Blue Branch. A combination Shell station, beer joint and grocery, it was also home to Hank Rudder and his wife, who lived upstairs. We'd stop in for a Coke so Dad could catch up with his old friend, walking through the double screen doors that advertised Rainbo Bread, no "w" in the name. We might find Hank leaning against the counter in a soiled butcher's apron, but he'd spring to life at the sight of my dad, laughing and carrying on even if the conversation nearly rolled over and died with the ongoing drought.

Under a thick haze of tobacco smoke and neon signs advertising Lone Star and Pearl beer, it wasn't uncommon to see a few locals absorbed in a game of dominoes. The head of a giant catfish, probably a state record, hung on a wall nearby. The building is deserted now, but in its heyday, Hank's Place was a hub of local commerce that kept him running through the screen doors to check on customers at the pumps and back in again to make change and open cans of beer using a church key before filling orders for the brisket and sausages he smoked in large brick pits out back. The first time I followed Dad to the smoking pits, I jumped at the sight of a stuffed bobcat that Hank had wired to a live-oak limb overhead, its teeth bared and ready to strike. On our way out, another bobcat stood frozen in time, snarling from one end of the counter.

Before the Austin bypass made a muddle of things, (and in my opinion *ruined* everything), we could spot the Blue Branch from the highway as we crested the next hill, the Perry Oak sitting like a giant sentinel holding up one corner of the white farmhouse, its red tin roof standing out like a postage stamp. Renters had been living there so long that the inside remained a mystery to me, but Mr. Roberts usually made an appearance, smiling and raising his pipe in greeting as we passed the house. Dad laid the groundwork about his childhood on the Blue Branch early on, romanticizing the place until it glowed with a magical aura. There was the time he lost his wristwatch and later found it under the Perry Oak after a fortune teller read some tea leaves; swimming in the buff and winter dunks in the blue hole with his two brothers; camping on the banks of the Colorado River; swinging from ancient grape vines at the creek just a few of the bedtime stories that kept us spellbound.

My first clear memory of the cabin is the smell of kerosene, musty quilts, and wormy wood, the guinea fowl scattering as we pulled alongside the cabin to park, my brother and I bursting from the car like lizards on hot rocks. While we helped Dad unload the car, mother started propping the windows open with sticks to give the room a good airing out. Mom and I wore pedal-pushers most of the year, and she'd wrap a red bandana around her head before sweeping cobwebs from every corner. Weather permitting, she liked to go barefoot, and sooner or later she'd stub a toe, holler a few faux curse words like "dad burn-it" and exclaim, "That's it, time for a cigarette break."

After Dad set out a few mouse traps, we left Mom sitting on the porch smoking a Kent and headed for La Grange to pick up lunch and supplies.

We always bought hot links and soda crackers at Prause's Market on the town square, the smoky aroma of mesquite hitting our noses just inside the front door. The sawdust floors and the separate eating area in back marked "Colored" fascinated me more than the deer trophies lining the walls or the sides of beef hanging in full view. Of course, all that silly business of separate eating spaces has changed since then, but the motherlode of hot links I devour on every visit, laced with the rich flavor of venison and garlic, hasn't varied one iota.

A historical marker denotes another hanging tree at one corner of the square that's been saved for posterity and protected from the encroachment of shops. The live oak, its trunk gnarled and patched with black tar, sits like an old relic that struggled up out of the concrete, lost a few limbs in the process, and may take its last breath any day. But the ancient tree, covered in lichens and mistletoe, never held that much interest for us. Ben and I were more interested in the icehouse, thinking of bygone days as Dad carried the twenty-pound block to the car with a pair of ice tongs, loading it into the trunk to feed the old metal ice box on the porch—old even then. We'd chip jagged chunks of ice for our drinks using a pick wedged in the door jam, taking turns emptying the gray enamel pan that caught the melt.

I'd always assumed the cabin had been built exclusively for us but found out years later that that was not the case. Some years before my grandparents moved to Houston, Granddad built the cabin for his field hands, a place they could congregate in the mornings, gather to eat lunch, or sing spirituals at the end of a long day chopping cotton, "Swing Low Sweet Chariot, "Wade in the Water," and "Steal Away to Jesus" among them. Emil Dove had tended his cotton crops over on Buckner's Creek in the early days but after a work-related accident left Emil blind in one eye, Granddad made him the caretaker of the ranch in their absence. Emil (Granddad pronounced it A-mill) had been a fixture in the family since my dad was a young boy. He enjoyed playing with Emil and Rosie's son, Lonnie. While my grandparents never spoke in derogatory tones about the Doves, the evening Dad straggled home well after suppertime, saying he'd taken supper with the Doves, they teased him unmercifully, laughing to themselves. Racial bias aside, my grandfather must have had a soft spot in his heart to set Emil up in the cabin with no visible means of support.

A stone's throw from the house, he built the cabin to match the house, with white lap siding, a tin roof, and double-hung windows all around.

I know Granddad couldn't help being a bigot. It's just the way he'd been raised. But something in Emil touched him, a kind of moxie that lived on through his many stories. The one I remember most vividly, the one Granddad took such delight in telling, was about the day Emil knocked on the back door of the Buckner Creek house asking if he could borrow a saw. Curious, my grandfather asked him what he needed with his saw.

"Well, Mr. Perry, the wife and me are breaking up housekeeping, and we can't agree on who gets the eatin' table. So to save any more arguments, I'm just gonna' saw the darn thing in half."

I don't think Emil and his wife were ever legally married. In the eyes of Texas, they'd be considered common law, or as Granddad put it, "They had a cotton-patch license." Emil lived out some of his golden years in solitude in the cabin, cooking on an open fire outside and listening to records on a small wind-up Victrola.

Eventually, the cabin evolved into a family getaway. A screen porch with a slab floor was added across the front. When the weather was pleasant, it made for a nice gathering place or additional sleeping quarters. Dove hunts and squirrel hunts were a family event in the early fall, and in the summer months we'd pick dewberries growing in wild abandon along the railroad tracks, or climb ladders to harvest the mustang grapes that still lace the treetops today.

The fifteen-by-twenty-foot room housed my grandmother's cast-off bedroom furniture where my folks slept in an old double bed with the footboard sawed off at a time when Hollywood beds—beds with no footboards—were the rage. Even then, I found it strange that Grandmother would deface a perfectly good bed in the name of fashion, but I enjoyed playing grown-up at her Darby vanity, poking through the drawers and pulling out old powder jars and discarded bottles of Evening in Paris cologne. My kid brother and I slept side-by-side on metal cots, and whenever a cold front blew in, as they invariably do in late fall or early spring, Dad fired up the kerosene heater to take the chill off the room while those old quilts pinned us down like lead aprons. Whenever a blue norther caught us off-guard, we bundled into the car and spent the night at the Carter Motel in town, passing the local juke joint along the way. A slatted privacy fence camouflaged the makeshift club, a place that always intrigued me as I caught a fleeting glimpse of a woman writhing as she danced.

At times the dust would aggravate my brother's asthma, and one weekend we'd forgotten to pack his nebulizer. As Benjie wheezed, my mother wheezed right along with him, gasping for breath while Dad made a hasty trip to the Hermes Drugstore in town, returning with some remedy the pharmacist recommended. He poured a grainy substance resembling sand from a small tin into one of my grandmother's old china saucers and lit it with a match. The grains fizzed and popped like a sparkler on the Fourth of July, filling the room with an acrid smoke he encouraged my brother to inhale. It seemed archaic at the time, but later that night I fell asleep to the sound of my brother's restful breathing.

Mom cooked a bacon-and-egg breakfast on a hot plate each morning, and in the evening we'd drag the red Chapman chairs from the porch and sit around an Old Smokey outside while Dad grilled steaks, waving to the caboose of every train that passed. We ate our meals on a pull-down table tucked into one corner of the room. Much like a Murphy bed, when locked in its upright position the table hides a wall cabinet of canned goods, something my grandfather built to conserve space. What really set the cabin apart from everything else was the little ecosystem going on in and around it. Mud dauber nests practically held the eaves of the porch together, and we got a hands-on lesson about the food chain after Dad cracked one open, revealing all the paralyzed insects sleeping inside.

It didn't take us long to settle into the quiet rhythms of country life. We lived among the rocks and the trees along the creek, a place surcharged with life and discovery, every step an adventure. Because of our proximity to the ground, there seemed to be an abundance of activity at our feet. We set out each morning carrying our Daisy BB guns, hot on the trail of anything that moved, stalking a dung beetle rolling a ball three times its size one minute, our attention drawn to an armadillo foraging in the brush the next, or a horned toad lapping up fat red ants on the nearest ant hill.

Following the ant trails that ran like threads from mound to mound and on to the dappled shade of a giant sycamore at the creek, we'd watch the cutter ants (atta Texana) make their way across the shallows on a flotilla of oak leaves while schools of minnows nibbled at the cracker-crumbs we'd toss their way. Beneath great rafts of Spanish moss, the Blue Branch gives off its own perfume: the sharp smell of cedars mixed with the dank odor of green algae floating in stagnant pools from one ledge to the next. Eventually, we'd wind on down to the blue hole and stand over the waterfall looking for any signs of life, especially at the entrance to a small cave, an irregular hole tunneled into the limestone ledge at the far end. Wildcat Cave featured in another of my father's boyhood yarns, and year after year we never lost hope of spotting the bobcat Dad claimed to have seen. The only bobcats we ever saw were the ones stuffed and mounted back at Hank's Place.

We never swam in the blue hole but loved to fish there, baiting our hooks with grasshoppers and dipping our corks into the murky green pool below us. Mother seemed happy enough to fry up our stringers of perch at the end of the day, and with our jeans covered in preacher's lice, we'd gather up the flattened pennies we'd set out on the railroad tracks that morning, returning to the cabin in happy exhaustion. Dad spent a lot of time with Ben and me, taking us hiking along the streambed of Cedar Creek and on to the river, pointing out a cottonwood tree along the way, or the native pecans, or the spiked bark of a tickle-tongue tree he said the Indians used for toothaches. We'd linger in the shade of an Osage orange tree, or bodark, taken from the French *bois d'arc*, meaning "bow wood," a reference to the Indians' use of the wood for archery bows. Livestock eat the nubby green hedge apples or "horse apples," which in our day were said to ward off household pests.

Sometimes Dad would take a shotgun along, clenching his jaw and making squabbling sounds to scare up the squirrels, bagging a few for supper along the way. As he watched us running along the sandy banks of the Colorado searching for buckeyes, catching frogs or skimming stones, I feel certain he was revisiting the best parts of his life there. But we couldn't imagine milking cows at four in the morning or straddling a log over a swollen creek to get to school. The closest we'd come to farm life in the city came in the form two chicks dyed red and green at Easter. If we ever tired of exploring the ranch, we'd crank up the Victrola and pick through the heavy brittle plates of music, playing a foxtrot or a polka, or Mom's favorite, "The Dixie War Hymn," complete with soldiers cheering in the background.

Through our college years, we deserted our little nirvana, and the cabin sat locked and idle until my brother married in 1976 and took up permanent residence in the big house a few years later. By that time the fire ants were so out of control they were crawling through the floorboards of the cabin in great droves. I shuddered the night we set the legs of my grandmother's old Hollywood bed in pans of water to keep the ants out.

I don't doubt that years of pesticide use, along with the fire ants, have played a role in the dwindling population of horned toads and their food supply. Although the chemical we once used was taken off the market, I can't remember the last time I saw a horned toad, a snake or even a tick, and generations of mud daubers have been lost. Today, my brother watches over the one red ant mound left between the house and the cabin. It's a huge gravel dome that just seems to rise out of the earth, and you have to side-step it to reach his back door. In an effort to keep the colony strong, he tosses out food scraps and says they're partial to cooked rice. It seemed obsessive at first, but who can argue with trying to save the last vestige of your childhood, even if it happens to be *ants*.

Nowadays, gecko lizards are taking over the cabin, another indication that the ecological balance has been turned upside down. They're a nuisance far worse than mice, and we set out sticky traps instead of poison to catch new clutches the old-timers call "rusty-guts" but so far, the rusty guts are winning. The old privy collapsed years ago and took the daddy long legs with it. It gave me the creeps during my childhood, but now that it's gone, I miss it.

Scissortail flycatchers don't range as far as the Carolinas, so whenever I spot one at the ranch there's something magical about it. In her memoir, *Cross Creek*, Marjorie Kinnan Rawlings says that we all need a place of enchantment. And roaming these grounds in the cool of a morning, picking Spanish moss, ball moss and yaupon holly to fashion into wreaths or standing over the blue hole to meditate brings with it a certain peace of mind. I think there's a connection to the places and things that fed your spirit growing up, for no matter what storms are brewing in my personal life, a visit to the cabin seems to be the miracle cure, if only temporarily.

I wish I could have known Emil Dove, heard him sing one of those spirituals, or seen his image in an old photograph. Did he listen to Muddy Waters or Blind Lemon Jefferson on his Victrola? The writer in me wants to know. My brother said he met him only once. That he was skinny as a rail and owned a horse named Red. And if Emil had had too much to drink at the juke joint up the road, Red knew the way home. Though Granddad paid him fifty dollars a month, a good wage at the time, the job as overseer didn't last. Mr. and Mrs. Roberts, tenants of the big house, were racially biased, and, feeling uncomfortable, Emil moved away.

I did have the good fortune of meeting a friend and co-worker of his one day during our drive from Houston. Riding a beautiful chestnut mare just ahead of us on Texas 71, the man jerked on the reins, waving his cowboy hat for us to pass. Dad pulled up alongside him, hanging out the window, all smiles as he said "Say, aren't you Jack McLaughlin?"

Jack, a big burly man with a booming voice, his caramel-colored skin glowing in the noonday sun, recognized Dad after a long minute. While they laughed and reminisced, my attention was drawn to that stub of a cigarette dangling from one corner of his mouth, an image that will always be with me, along with the jingle- jangle of his silver spurs.

Emil would marvel at the new and improved version of his old homestead. Though we've added a bathroom, kitchenette, and bunk room, we still prop the windows open with sticks and lock the front door with the original skeleton key. Future generations won't share the same experiences I've had, but close friends know it's where I long to be whenever life throws me a curve. Upon my arrival, I'll turn off my cell phone and tuck it away. I'll hike the grounds looking for any signs of mud daubers, cutter ants or horned toads, taking in the intoxicating aromas of the creek. Eventually, friends passing through will catch up with me, for despite all the changes, it's still a place of restful breathing. ✦

Left to Right: Kerry, Cathy, Lexi and Baby Ben
Photo taken at Village of Yesteryear, Houston, TX, 1977

Chapter 2 – The Big House

The house is part of the whole
Cohesive world we live in.

— PAUL'S HILL BY SHELBY STEPHENSON

I was a young mother with a baby in diapers and a husband fighting a useless war in Vietnam the first time I set foot inside the craftsman bungalow my grandparents built circa 1929. The big house, as we've come to call it, had been a dream of my grandparents long in the making, and seeing the interior for the first time brought with it a fluid sequence of family events.

Dad, who was nine at the time, remembers the planning and preparation as his parents argued over which direction to point the front of the house: toward the proposed highway yet to come, or toward the upper pasture. In the end, the house was built in the shade of the live oak and faces the pasture. It was wired for electricity at a time when there was none to be had in rural areas; cooking on a kerosene stove and living by the light of kerosene lamps was the norm until my father enrolled at Texas A&M in the late 1930s. Though my grandparents had torn down the existing house before building the new one, they left the detached kitchen in the dooryard for storage purposes. A small wood-frame building that rests on sandstone blocks, its ashen walls sandblasted by time, it remains untouched since the turn of the century.

After they relocated to Houston, my grandparents rented out the big house with the understanding that family members would be free to visit, have use of the cabin, and hunt on the property. Mr. and Mrs. Roberts were the only renters I ever knew, a pleasant, easygoing couple with a flock of guinea hens always underfoot, renters I only knew from a distance throughout my childhood. After the Roberts retired and moved out, Dad's older brother, Uncle Fred, and his wife, Sue, moved in. They'd lived in many far-flung places from Odessa, Texas to Hobbs, New Mexico, places we once traveled to for family visits. They'd just relocated from Dallas, and it was good to reconnect with my cousin Eileen and her husband. Sue still carried a big chip on her shoulder, which brought to mind the last weekend I'd spent visiting Eileen during our teen years. We'd fixed beef stroganoff for supper, and I'd set the table with some dinner plates that hadn't been used for some time. Apparently, the dishes were laden with dust, and there was no end to the ragging I received from Aunt Sue.

None of us could have foreseen the rockslide that was coming, our sporadic visits always met with surprises, the cabin rendered uninhabitable after Uncle Fred boarded up the screen porch to the point you couldn't sit and enjoy the view, not to mention all the paraphernalia they'd stuffed inside. I don't know why or exactly when life soured for my aunt and uncle, but over time, the situation deteriorated rapidly. For the next ten years nobody felt welcome, their alcoholism surfacing after we spent a few harrowing weekends in the cabin. My aunt would curse at us through a back window, using words hot enough to raise a blister. Getting poleaxed any time we strayed too close to the house was one thing, Sue's belittling Uncle Fred in front of my grandparents was the last straw. When I confronted Eileen about her mother, she said to ignore her, but it was hard to ignore the scathing outbursts coming from a woman who claimed to be a direct descendant of Chief Sitting Bull.

The last straw came the day Granddad stopped by to pick up some well water. Aunt Sue met him at the well and told him that his son was a miserable failure, adding a few more derogatory comments before walking away. It was a dark time for all concerned and posed a family dilemma: how to get them out gracefully. At some point, a local realtor offered to buy the Blue Branch at a good price. When Granddad sounded interested, my grandmother phoned Dad, fretting about the possibility of losing their beloved Blue Branch, a place they'd worked so hard to obtain. That's when my sister-in-law planted the seed that spurred us on to keep the place in the family.

Though none of us could afford to buy it outright, Cathy suggested in wheeler-dealer fashion that we pool our resources. After many conversations and some coaxing on her part, my parents, Ben and Cathy and yours truly bought the Blue Branch collectively in a sweetheart deal, my grandparents transferring the deed to us, thus ending the reign of terror.

Uncle Fred and Aunt Sue didn't stray too far, however, living out their lives in a mobile home on the Munch property next door, where I'm sure my aunt kept an evil eye on all the comings and goings at the Blue Branch, which would account for that feeling of always being watched.

My brother and sister-in-law hadn't really planned on living at the Blue Branch. They'd already bought some land in San Marcos and started building a house there. But Mom and Dad, ever the clinging vines, had been going through separation anxiety about their move. After some jockeying, Ben and Cathy sold the San Marcos property and moved their expanding family into the big house.

Things went smoothly for a time. Ben and Cathy lived the hippie life of *right livelihood*, Cathy seemingly the yin to his yang, chatty and outgoing, a real chatterbox compared to his reserved nature. They planted a large vegetable garden, raised rabbits and chickens, and harvested honey from their beehives. Ben set up his wood-wright shop in the barn, his stereo speakers up in the rafters, his radio set to KLBJ out of Austin while he worked, honing his craft with every stroke of a brush or the gentle tap of a dovetail joint as he restored furniture for various locals, at one point building a display cabinet for a business in town. He also helped Cathy with the tropical-plant business she still maintained in Houston, doing deliveries and installations when needed.

At long last, the Big Sleep at the Blue Branch ended as cattle and horses, a piglet named Easter, and a couple of wooly sheep, one called Foda, roamed the grounds, all thanks to Ben and Cathy. And decades before Martha Stewart would become a household name, Cathy's Araucana hens were laying pastel-colored eggs. The empty tack room filled up with saddles, bridles and gear while Sugar, the gray Arabian mare with the sweet disposition gave birth to a black colt named Dewdrop, who arrived in the early- morning dew. Later on, another foal, Midnight, was born at the stroke of midnight. Pinecone had her first litter of kittens. and Cathy's Irish wolfhound had a litter of pups. Everything seemed to be breeding simultaneously, the Blue Branch crawling with life. On weekend visits my heart beat with the joyful notes of an airy piano concerto as I drove around the sweep of gravel and parked beneath the Perry Oak. At long last the white lap-sided house had opened up for all of us, and my grandparents could take pleasure in walking the grounds again. The rooms exhaled laughter and remembrance, a feeling of exuberance filling the air.

Cathy created a sunspot at the end of the driveway, planting three cabbage palms between the house and the cabin. That first Christmas, I bought a brass sundial for its center that read *Tempus Fugit*, or time flies. She had her own ideas about the vegetable garden as well. For instance, if you plant rows of corn with beans and squash in between, the beans will magically twine up the corn stalks, replenishing the nitrogen the corn takes away from the soil while the broad, prickly leaves of the squash vines repel pesky insects, a thing Native Americans had been doing for centuries and a process the early colonists called the Three Sisters.

We used the back door most of the time, the kitchen just off the dining room painted a buttery yellow. All the rooms sparkled with fresh coats of pastel paint, shiny brass ceiling fans whirring overhead. I pictured my father and his brothers shooing the flies from the dining room before closing all the windows at suppertime. The dining room opened into a spacious living area flanked by the master bedroom and a large room my father shared with his two brothers. Previous tenants walked away with most of the family treasures stored in the walk-up attic, but we went through the old trunks anyway just to see what scraps we might find, like the old stereoscopic viewer and the standup Victrola now on display in the living room. The epitome of *carpe diem*, Cathy seized each day with visions for the place that seemed endless that first year as a wood stove sprang up in one corner of the dining room, an old upright piano in another. Ben could hardly keep up, for as soon as he finished building a large greenhouse in the front pasture, she was planning an enormous sunroom off to one side of the house with a master bath featuring a bidet and a lap pool outside. Most of us look for the art within ourselves, but after hearing Cathy's plans, my folks struggled to keep the farmhouse looking like a farmhouse instead of a missile silo or something that resembled a miniature Hearst Castle with wings and turrets running in all directions. But Cathy had never been hindered by convention, and one day during a quiet moment with my brother, Dad referred to Cathy as "that crazy woman." My brother's reply: "Well, that crazy woman is my *wife*."

While I spruced up the cabin, painting my grandmother's old kitchen chairs a cobalt blue and adding small bluebonnets and a BB logo to the back of each one, Cathy was already in the throes of hatching a new project: damming up a section of the creek at the bottom of the slope behind the house to create a large pond. Dad was skeptical at first, as was his nature. None of us knew quite how to take her. We weren't accustomed to such vision. I believe she could have persuaded the Eskimos into abandoning their igloos under the pretense they're depleting the polar ice cap, delicate as a stick of dynamite while trying to prove a point. She did manage to raise Dad's consciousness in the end, though I wondered about the sanity of this endeavor as the demolition crew arrived and several grand old live oaks were bulldozed in the process.

Once the pond came into being, an acre of sparkling green water, pretty as a picture, Cathy was determined to raise freshwater shrimp. Her entrepreneurial side clashed with Dad's practical side, so he ignored the request, stocking the pond with smallmouth bass and channel cats, adding a short pier and a rowboat later on. At any rate, Cathy got her Walden Pond, a laconic place to meditate, fish, and commune with nature. And everyone seemed satisfied, though a few repercussions arose that had to be dealt with. Locals can get pretty worked up about their land, and Gus Friemel, who lived on the other side of the creek, called one day in deep agitation, complaining that the headwaters of the Blue Branch backed up onto his property during a heavy downpour. I kept thinking *lawsuit* all the while, but felt confident that Dad-the-surveyor knew all the legal ramifications beforehand, and thankfully, that episode blew over.

The other misfire with the pond came gradually. Although the concrete spillway remained dry, with a miniscule flow of water throughout the year, in the event of a gully-washer, a great many fish washed over it and on to the swimming hole, then out to Cedar Creek, and on to the Colorado River, silt washing in with each successive flood and raising the depth. To add insult to injury, over time, the pond became a perfect breeding ground for an aquatic plant called hydrilla, a pest Ben and Dad spent countless hours treating with a heavy syrup-like dye to block out the sun's rays, a process that had to be repeated after each gully-washer.

Over time, a thick stand of cattails sprouted (seemingly overnight) at the far end of the pond like an army guarding the West Bank. And until we managed to beat back the fire ants, they found a haven at water's edge, lining up along the banks, ready to sting the unwary. Though there was no evidence of it at our pond, there had been reports of a deadly brain-eating amoeba, *Naegleria fowleri*, that had sprung up in other ponds across the state, which gave me pause, and Cathy as well, whenever the kids wanted to swim.

Through it all, there was the ever-present sound of children at play, scurrying through the house or shrieking in the background as they jumped on the trampoline or raced their tricycles down the slope to the pond. But, as we've already seen, country life isn't without its pitfalls. During the winter months, the wood stove belched great clouds of black smoke. After knocking out the stovepipe, it was rock solid with creosote from burning green wood. Then one wintry night the greenhouse burned down after a large ficus tree toppled, knocking over a kerosene heater. Upsetting, sure, but Cathy seemed more distraught over the loss of her bougainvillea vines. Plants must have been her first love, for I'd watched her any number of times as she spent meticulous hours pruning and trimming some raggedy palms and dracaenas with the patience of a brain surgeon, hoping to revive them in the greenhouse for use in her plant rental business.

Before Ben and Cathy met, she made trips in her VW Camper, venturing deep into the interior of Mexico and on to the Yucatan to collect orchids and bromeliads. When I found out Cathy's father was a retired admiral, I wondered if she'd picked up the wanderlust gene from him. Traveling to the far-flung Mayan ruins of Palenque and Tulum with her daughter, Lexi, in tow, she embraced the Mexican culture and picked up the language like a summer song. It certainly wasn't my forte, but I admired her hugely for going where few young, single mothers have gone before, setting her own course and living life on her own terms.

I first met Cathy inside her Houston greenhouse where she was busy watering some tillandsia plants, silvery brush-like orbs suspended from the ceiling on bits of driftwood. When I asked what they were, she replied jokingly, "Until they bloom, I call them shitz-a-lots-a, because they look like shit, and there's a lot of them."

I found that we had some things in common, namely Carlos Castaneda and house plants. Though I enjoyed house plants, I didn't consider myself a green thumb back then, or for that matter an authority on the Yaqui brand of "seeing."

But Cathy wanted to expand her business using "synergy, and when she offered me a job, I jumped at the chance. I'd been working for a high-powered insurance agent who had the personality of JR Ewing, and the stress had become intolerable. We made a good team. Ideas and sales were her strong points, problem-solving and organization mine. My father came up with a business slogan, "Don't get caught with your plants down," and we spent long, muggy days driving around Houston in her Toyota station wagon, making infrequent trips to a wholesaler called Magic Valley, a greenhouse run by a friendly hippie couple out the Gulf Freeway where I learned the difference between a chamedorea palm and a massangeana cane.

There wasn't much to it, really. We knocked on office doors, gave our sales pitch, installed plants, and made weekly rounds to care for them. During our maintenance rounds I watched a sales pro in action as Cathy explained to customers that our plants "thrived on neglect," something she repeated with utmost zeal at every stop. She taught me so much, like removing spent or dead leaves from a plant to heighten the plant's energy. Up until then I didn't know plants had energy. I took a cut in pay, but it was liberating to say good-bye to tight-fitting pantyhose and say hello to casual footwear. My flexible schedule gave me the freedom of a stay-at-home-mom, and for the first time in my life I felt like I had some control over my own destiny. Our days began with getting the kids off to school during the *Phil Donahue Show* and ended with sweaty brows and dirt under our fingernails. We waltzed through the board rooms of Mega Law Firms, Big Oil Companies, Swedish Corporations, and Japanese Conglomerates. And with Cathy's finesse, we could have walked back out with enough trade secrets to rock the state. We held an occasional "recycled" plant sale for our customers, squeezing every last nickel from our investment. Cathy was my alter-ego. I never would have made the leap without her.

As soon as Cathy found out their rental house in Houston was scheduled for demolition, she and Ben drove there and dug up a truckload of shrubs, digging and digging and digging until they'd planted every last one along the barb wire fence at the tracks. But the wax leaf ligustrums, antique roses, and azalea bushes were no match for the harsh summer sun or the buck-shot soil of the ranch, dying a slow, agonizing death, reduced to skeletons by summer's end.

City folk who move to the country aren't always prepared for a sudden turn of events. You settle in and get comfortable with day-to-day life until the unforeseen happens. When chicken snakes appeared in the henhouse, Uncle Fred, who remained cordial despite the unexpected move, was always happy to relieve Cathy of the chore of obliteration with his .410 shotgun, although the nest of copperheads Ben and Dad gunned down inside the smokehouse was a much worse threat. Webworms destroyed an old beehive and fire ants killed some baby rabbits in their cages. There were mounting vet bills beginning with a cow in a breach birth situation, and Midnight needed a horse whisperer to break him of charging at people and biting their behinds. Come spring, the rooster took to attacking the kids and ended up on our dinner plates. Sometime after that, an impromptu graveyard set out in a far corner of the lower pasture held the remains of pets felled on the railroad tracks with numbing regularity.

Dove hunts had always been an annual rite of passage in our growing-up years, so one spring Ben planted the lower pasture in giant sunflowers for the hunt the coming fall. But Cathy hated the very idea of guns around children, emphasizing to anybody who'd listen that mourning doves mate for life. While the pasture shimmered like hammered gold in the late afternoon sun, the summer wind igniting the field like a runaway prairie fire, guns became a sore point. Wolves had been spotted in the area and posed a real threat to the livestock, and my brother ribbed Cathy that she wouldn't be satisfied until he tied pretty red bows around their necks. You couldn't ignore her complaints, but trying to pacify her was like bagging hornets. By the time the sunflowers nodded their great blackened heads toward the ground and dove season drew nigh, their differences had reached a fever pitch.

Though Dad had initially resisted the idea of buying the Blue Branch, saying he'd probably never utilize it much, he commissioned my brother to add an addition to the cabin: a small bunk room and adjoining bathroom. And as soon as the last fixture was in place, my parents became fixtures there every weekend. I sometimes wondered if that wasn't too much togetherness, and the day came when Cathy grew restless, approaching us about buying the big house and the land under it. But the layout of the property doesn't lend itself easily to division, and Dad, as a surveyor, tried to explain that there was no good place for another right-of-way from the highway, that the railroad tracks splitting the house and outbuildings from the lower pasture posed problems. The new pond and the blue hole were other mitigating factors, and after we nixed the idea, there was an underlying current of tension between us.

The situation had all the makings of a Steinbeck saga as the big house became a pawn in an ongoing game of chess. And like in chess, it soon grew apparent that we'd reached a stalemate. None of us are picture postcards of perfection, but a round of counseling failed to resolve their differences, and Cathy left Ben, moving to a house in town with Lexi and little Ben. I guess we all saw their split coming, but it was a painful thing to watch. I felt sorry for my brother, but it's always the kids who suffer the most when couples divorce. And little Ben took it very hard, shedding tears any time we were together. My feelings were jumbled as well. It felt like a pox had taken over the place. The vegetable garden went to seed, a healthy stand of Johnson grass crowding out the vegetables, the unfinished addition to the house sitting idle, the rain and weather beating through its empty interior. Poor Foda, unshorn since day one, ran around on little stick legs, her wooly coat so thick I thought she might collapse under the weight. Midnight was set free to roam, a common sight to see him on the front porch, his head thrust inside an open window, curtains flapping in the breeze like neglected laundry. Through the ensuing years the house lost its patina, a kind of shabbiness taking over. The white picket fence collapsed from old age, a network of Saint Augustine burying the limestone path out front as the pond threatened to dry up despite years of maintenance.

Flash forward about twenty years. Cathy has since remarried and traded in her plant business for a Realtor's license, flipping houses in Houston. Early one day, she stops by with her husband Steve. They've come to take in the Shakespeare Festival in Round Top a few miles away, dropping off my nephew, Taylor, born a month after the separation. That she and my brother are on speaking terms feels like a small miracle. And while my son, Kerry, is sorting through junk and treating termites in the old corn crib, the honey extractor and a chicken feeder surface. If seeing these relics from the past makes Ben and Cathy feel awkward, I don't pick up on it. Somewhat tentatively, Cathy joins him in the barn where he shows off his latest projects, restoring an old cedar chest and the beginnings of a hope chest he's building for his stepdaughter, Lexi, a doctor now engaged to another doctor from La Grange.

My brother is a perfectionist and a master at his craft, his shop a jumble of routers, planers, sanders and old hand tools. Some of the best gifts he ever gave me came from his shop. The hull of a sizeable boat hewn from Osage orange he started in the early days, a wood that's practically indestructible if left in the elements, sits unfinished at one end of the barn. When they were first married, he took in antiques for restoration, still every bit the artisan, though I think Cathy's hope was that one day he'd graduate from dovetail joints and join the ranks of James Surls, a Texas artist known for his wood sculptures. I couldn't help but wonder what was running through their minds during her visit.

Whenever my nephews come around, the big house feels uplifted and joyful. Under their father's tutelage, they've become skilled marksmen, and in due course, the house resembles a small arsenal during hunting season, the well-riffled pages of a Cabela's catalogue always within reach. With links of venison sausage on the horizon, the kitchen spins with culinary delights as my brother-the-chef cooks their favorite foods.

Love, like life, is as fragile as the air we breathe. And time is the great healer.

Chapter 3 – The Cinderella Beauty Shop

Genius is of small use to a woman who does not know how to do her hair.
— EDITH WHARTON

I suppose most everyone has a special place, a retreat if you will, where you can unwind, relax, and meditate, a place that feeds the spirit. It might be the bend in a river or a bird sanctuary or a tranquil path through a wooded park. For my grandmother, it was her beauty shop.

In the days and months following their move to the Blue Branch, the tension between my grandmother and her mother-in-law had been steadily growing. When my widowed great-grandmother, Mary Eve, moved into the farmhouse, occupying the back bedroom built to accommodate her, an age-old problem sprouted: how to get along with a cantankerous mother-in-law. Though she died before I was born, I felt like I knew her from my father's stories, few of them good. Let it be said that during my growing-up years, Granddad never had anything negative to say about his mother. And my grandmother, Elsie, never spoke of Mary Eve at all.

The fact that my grandmother was a third-generation German may have played a part in Mary Eve's revolt, though it went further than

23

that. A Bible-thumping Southern Baptist who never approved of my grandparents' love of dancing, or the fact they'd joined the Methodist Church, Mary Eve would throw a hissy fit any time she caught wind they were heading out to a dance, screaming at my grandmother that she was leading her son straight into the fires of Hell and reducing her three grandsons to tears before the tirade ended.

Though my grandparents were teetotalers for the most part, come summertime, they did like to pick the mustang grapes that grow wild on the property, making jellies and jams, along with a small amount of grape wine for special occasions. Naturally, this didn't sit well with Granny Eve, who could be sly as a fox and equally crafty when trying to prove a point. The situation reached a fever pitch the day Ivan, Elsie, and their three boys drove into town to run some errands, leaving Granny Eve behind. In their absence, she marched down the path that runs between the house and the workshop and found the crocks of wine fermenting there on a shelf. It was my father who discovered the open spigots later in the day, reporting the mess to his forlorn mother. I can only imagine the scene that must have taken place as I picture the dank-smelling purple ooze covering the concrete floor of the workshop and the fireworks that surely followed.

To be fair, Mary Eve had had her share of hard knocks in life. She never knew her parents. They died when she was a baby, leaving her mother's sister, Aunt Laurinda, and her husband to raise her alongside their five children. While I feel sure she had a good life with them, there were some aching wounds to follow in her married life. Mary Eve and my great-grandfather, William, raised four boys on the Blue Branch, but their third son, Roy, had been a sickly child, suffering from an asthmatic condition that caused his early death. According to his death certificate, he succumbed to pneumonia at the age of twenty. And seven years after their son Pomp returned unscathed from the trenches of World War I, their firstborn son, Kurt, a fireman for the Southern Pacific Lines, was killed in a freak train accident when the engine derailed. He jumped from the speeding train on the spur of the moment, his skull crushed when he hit the hard ground. The engine ran a little further and turned on its side with the engineer and brakeman still in the cab. They crawled out unhurt, but the sudden stop of the gravel cars caused the gravel to spill, Kurt's body completely covered. He left a wife and two small children behind, a boy and a girl, the youngest only six months, a family tragedy that made the local paper. Though Granddad had told me about the circumstances surrounding the loss of his brother, I ran across the *La Grange Journal*'s account on microfilm many years later. Reading it certainly put a lump in my throat.

A little more than a year after Kurt's death, The Grim Messenger called once more when her beloved husband William succumbed to pneumonia and died. It must have been the worst kind of loneliness. I think Mary Eve turned to her religion for solace, for answers, fearing if she strayed too far from the Baptist creed or the Bible, she'd be struck down yet again. But religion can do funny things to people. And while I'm sure my grandmother felt some compassion for Mary Eve, after Elsie's world got pared down, she needed to find a resolution to the upper-level disturbance that had overtaken the household.

Though they were both good Christian women, each saw the world through a different lens, and when the situation became unbearable, Elsie decided to find a solution. To keep the peace and make the best of things, she decided to enroll in a beautician's school in San Antonio, taking the train from Schulenburg every Monday morning and living with her sister, Tillie, and Tillie's husband, Charlie, during the week, returning to the Blue Branch on Friday afternoons. Stout-hearted as she was, I feel certain she left the house each Monday morning like an animal just set free from a steel trap, her boys old enough to fend for themselves, my father driving her to and from the railroad depot in dutiful fashion.

By the time I was old enough to accompany my grandmother on visits in the 1950s, the kitchen of Tillie's house in Alamo Heights was always Food Central. On any given day there'd be ice cream churning in the sink, loaves of bread baking in the oven, and pots on every burner of the stove. Charlie Decker, her second husband, was a railroad man of good humor who was partial to cigars. Swamp coolers in the windows, a form of evaporative cooling, kept the house comfortable on the hottest summer days.

Tillie and Elsie had always been kindred spirits. Both were fun-loving women, Elsie with her high-pitched giggle, Tillie's laughter more of a cackle. Aunt Tillie reminded me of a Rudolph Dirks cartoon, her

Dutchy speech, along with her hair, which she wore in a knot on top of her head, a carryover from the old country, the two of them always in stitches over something. I found out from a census dated 1910 that Tillie's Christian name was Otilia, Elsie's, Elsa, their names getting Americanized between the two Great Wars, Elsa cutting her ties to the homeland one by one. Even so, she called me her little *schnickelfritz* from time to time, a German endearment.

I don't know where the idea for her shop originated, whether she found an ad in the paper or had an epiphany, but after she received her beautician certification, she rented a space on the second floor of the Streithoff building on the town square, just down the way from the Fashion Shop, one of her favorite haunts. She had a telephone installed, delighted with this new form of communication, though it would be years before they could get one at the farmhouse. As she painted and decorated, gaining customers week by week, the Cinderella Beauty Shop soon became her little oasis, her escape. She'd finally found her glass slipper, entirely free, at least for a while, from the dark energy of her mother-in-law. Or, as my father put it, "They got out of each other's hair."

In recent years, while working on a book about Granny Eve and her life on the Blue Branch, my father pointed out the exact location of the shop on the north side of the square. The next morning, after I'd spent an hour at the Heritage Center unravelling family history, I climbed to the top of the steep staircase just off the sidewalk. It was one of those clear, crisp spring days people in Texas live for, and I peered through the glass door to that empty space wondering what Cinderella's must have looked like back in the day. A bank of windows looks out to the courthouse with its manicured lawn and majestic oaks, dappled sunlight cascading across the hardwood floors in irregular patterns.

I knew my grandmother intimately. I knew her favorite color was powder blue. I knew about her love of songbirds and the canary she kept at the ranch house. I knew she liked fine things: costume jewelry, stylish hats, satin shoes, silk stockings, McCoy pottery, and China figurines. A trio of her Gould bird prints hang in my great room, soft pastels of cockatoos, love birds, and parakeets.

I remember when I wanted a parakeet for my tenth birthday. But my mother said I couldn't have one and she wasn't backing down. The day

Granny called and asked me what I wanted, I hadn't meant to pit them against each other. I just wanted a blue parakeet like any other normal ten-year-old. On the day of my party, I'd given up hope, down in the dumps as my friends filed in with their gifts. Then I heard a car door slam and looked out the window. There was Granny strutting across our lawn carrying a bright yellow bird cage. Mother was livid, and the minute she opened the door, she and Granny locked horns. When Mother confronted her, Granny said that if I'd asked for a donkey, she would have bought me one. It was one birthday party I'll never forget. Elsie was a ball of energy, always busy, always in motion, and I'm sure she "hit the floor running" when it came to the Cinderella Beauty Shop, turning it into a shop that would rival the best salons Houston or San Antonio had to offer. Aside from the utilitarian sinks, mirrors and paraphernalia, in my mind's eye I see wicker furniture upholstered in a bright floral fabric; my grandmother had a passion for fashion and liked nothing better than feathering her nest.

Long before we knew about her beauty shop, she'd take me and my cousin Pam to fashion shows at Sakowitz Brothers in downtown Houston, the *crème de la crème* of department stores until Neiman Marcus came on the scene years later. Granny always dressed to the nines, a shawl of mink pelts draped around her shoulders in cooler weather. We'd lunch in the tearoom, dining on dainty finger sandwiches as models skinny as mannequins paraded across the runway, hips thrust forward, a quick pirouette as Granny nodded her approval. On our way out, we'd stop at the Estee Lauder counter so she could replenish her supply of facial creams, following her outside in a wake of Youth Dew perfume as we crossed the street to Foley's, where school clothes for two growing girls were more affordable.

I can picture a coffee table with magazines neatly stacked, *Vogue* and *Harper's Bazaar* among them. Her secretary desk is up front, the one my father built for her in woodshop, the one she later gave to me chock full of bills and receipts, the *La Grange Journal* open to the latest sales and dance ads, a box of pastel stationary and a fountain pen for letters to her three sisters scattered across the state. There are potted plants on small accent tables in each window, for she had an affinity for plants of every description: a Boston fern, a pot of hen and chicks, an aloe or a snake plant. And because she was an accomplished seamstress, she'd made a batch of colorful aprons to wear while she worked. Perhaps, during a lull in her day, she'll pick up her basket of tatting, or crochet some doilies for those tabletops.

Leaving the house each morning and setting out for town must have felt like a jail break. And I like to think that Cinderella's served as a meeting place after hours where she and Granddad could visit quietly in late afternoons after he'd finished his railroad shift, helping her sweep the floors or tally up the day's receipts and make the bank deposit. Perhaps when the occasion presented itself, they'd take in a movie at the Cozy Theatre, catching the *Gold Diggers of 1933*, or *The Thin Man* with Myrna Loy and William Powell, dressed to the nines. And if Baca's Band or the Blume Orchestra were playing somewhere close by, they'd secretly change clothes and sneak off to a dance in Round Top or Swiss Alp, Granny Eve none the wiser. The boys could cover for them if need be, having taken part since they were toddlers, a pallet set out in a corner of the dance floor, learning the steps to the schottische early on: *Kleindeutchland*, or Little Germany, was still alive and well in the Texas Hill Country.

When her three boys dropped by the shop after school, Elsie would give them her undivided attention between appointments, free from the constant scrutiny of Old Ironsides. On occasion, she'd meet one of them in the atrium of the courthouse and share a leisurely lunch of salami sandwiches. Or maybe little Ivan, always a finicky eater, would stop by and complain about the lunch at school and she'd indulge him with a quarter so he could eat a bowl of stew at the Bon Ton Café. And from her crow's nest above the square, as her boys got older, she could watch them as they circled the courthouse on their Harleys, gunning their engines as they went. Daddy said that one day a customer and local busy body wondered aloud who the noisemakers belonged to. "Those are *my* boys," Elsie replied. I can see her saying this with a devilish grin and a quick tilt of her head, one of those little moments she'd relive at the supper table that evening.

Elsie possessed a good head for business, two of her many mantras being "It takes money to make money," and "It's not *what* you know, but *who* you know." But I'm still astounded, what with the Great Depression years dragging on, that she'd been so successful with Cinderella's that she later opened another shop in the little backwater town of Fayetteville, some fifteen miles away as the crow flies. She named that shop Cleopatra's, but it was not without its problems. Vivacious and outgoing, Elsie attracted many friends from the Methodist Ladies Auxiliary the Eastern Star, and the local Garden Club.

She'd hired a young beautician to run the Fayetteville shop, but over time, had grown suspicious about the daily receipts not adding up, falling short. I'm sure there'd been some small-town gossip leading up to her distrust, but if there was one thing Elsie wouldn't tolerate it was out-and-out theft. Her dilemma was just how to catch out the new employee and prove the theft. One of her friends came to her rescue, suggesting that Elsie send a few close friends over to Cleopatra's and get various services, say a wash and style, or a permanent wave, then report back to her, after which Elsie would check what the bank deposit totaled that day. Apparently, they set up the caper quite well, for, sure enough, just as my grandmother had suspected, the receipts that day fell short, and when confronted, the new beautician confessed. And that was the end of Cleopatra's. Grandmother decided she didn't need the angst of trying to find honest help and tame a tempest at home at the same time.

(There's another branch of the family tree who wouldn't agree with my father's harsh portrayal of Granny Eve. But it's a small branch, a twig really, so I stand firm with his assessment, a man who, after all, lived with his grandmother and mother all those years.)

The Cinderella Beauty Shop would thrive well into the 1940's, long after Granny Eve finally got the state pension she'd been waiting for and moved into a boarding house in town. The business had served its purpose, the gauntlet tossed long ago, the only proof it ever existed coming from the stories my father handed down to me, along with my grandmother's penchant for styling my hair in finger waves or a French twist or a Toni Perm that made my eyes water as she dabbed ammonia onto those tiny plastic curlers. The only tangible reminders left of those days is a small wooden plaque Dad made for his mother with his wood-burning kit, etching the name Cinderella's at the top, with the profile of an attractive young woman sporting a wavy bob from the Flapper era, and that vacant space on the second floor of the Streithoff building.

Mary Eve died in the fall of 1940, joining the "greater majority," as the *La Grange Journal* put it. Tough as sphere metal to the end, in her will, she left her estate, a small ranch over on Buckner's Creek, to her son, Pomp, Granddad's older brother, taking one last swipe at my grandparents from the grave. ❧

Grandmother Elsie Perry, 1956

Chapter 4 – Cool, Clear Water

...if only they too could hear the hum of honeybees singing from the hollow
In a grove where their fathers and their fathers' fathers stopped
To drink from springs that are cool and clear and deep, tinged
With bittersweetness that defies time and place and memory.

— TEXAS POETRY CALENDAR 2015 BY MARGARET DORNAUS

My grandfather spent the first nine years of his life on the Blue Branch picking cotton elbow-to-elbow with ex-slaves. During that time, my great-grandparents, William and Mary Eve, had been renting the place, chopping cotton and scraping by until they could buy a farm of their own. After they relocated to a hardscrabble ranch on the other side of town, and in all the years he spent away from that hallowed ground, Granddad kept his eye on the prize.

At the age of sixteen, he met the love of his life at a church social during a game of "Drop your handkerchief on a moonlit night." Granddad, a tall, lanky redhead with piercing blue eyes, was of Scotch-Irish descent; my grandmother was an attractive brunette of German stock. He said it was love at first sight, that he was drawn to her because she didn't talk "Dutchy" like so many young women in the area, plus she had a wonderful sense of humor. After they "jumped the broom," eloping at the tender ages of sixteen and fifteen respectively, Granddad took to calling her his little girl, a nickname that stuck for the duration of their married life. They too rented a patch of land with a house, once again chopping cotton on Bucker's Creek.

"In those days a silver dollar looked as big as a wagon wheel," he'd say. "We were so poor that at suppertime we'd hang a piece of meat from the ceiling, stand on a chair and swallow it before we jumped down."

I'm guessing that was an exaggeration, but after a few good years in cotton, at a time when cotton was king, they had saved enough money to purchase the Blue Branch, moving into their newly built house with their three boys, my father celebrating his ninth birthday there.

 "Mama used to say that farmers have more faith in God than any group of people on earth. Even so, I was glad to get out of it," Granddad was fond of saying.

Although they ran a dairy and grew cotton and corn during the Depression years, my grandparents knew they needed a more stable source of income. Through a stroke of luck, a job opened up with the Southern Pacific Railroad. My grandfather felt lucky to get it. "Every cow man goes broke three times in his life," he'd say. "You can go bust in the quickest possible time. One year you might be in high cotton, the next year you might get what they called bumblebee cotton, cotton so feeble and low to the ground a bumblebee could lie on its back and kick the locks right out of the bolls. And I ain't even mentioned the boll weevil or subterranean prices."

Granddad had big hands and a big heart. My mother served her iced tea unsweetened for Sunday dinner and I'd watch him as he spooned sugar into his glass, stirring and stirring with those working man's hands until his goblet resembled a snow globe. He was low-key, but spoke with authority on any subject, never in a hurry to get anywhere, a man who rarely raised his voice. He was a proud Texan through and through, so it didn't surprise me much the day he opened the morning paper to find that Alaska had become a state, slamming the paper to the floor, red-faced as he declared that if all the ice in Alaska melted, Texas would still be the biggest. He was equally as proud and protective about the Blue Branch, a place hard-won and never without its difficulties.

After he retired from the railroad and they settled in Houston, Granddad made weekly trips to La Grange in his mint green Ford pickup to get a haircut, visit family and friends, and pick up a few dozen yard eggs or a slab of bacon with the rind on it. Before he left town he'd take lunch at the Bon Ton Café, making one last stop at the Blue Branch to collect the rent and check his cattle. Donning a Panama hat to protect his fair skin, he'd stand beneath the massive limbs of the Perry Oak, thinking back to the April night in 1910 when his mother woke him from exhausted sleep and he stumbled out to the pasture with his three older brothers to take in Halley's Comet. "Momma said that since I was the youngest, if I lived to be an old man, I had a fair chance of seeing the comet again."

It's a story he enjoyed telling from time to time even though his mother possessed a hornet's disposition and rarely engaged in jollification, a living, breathing Texas tornado when it came to abiding by the Scripture and leading the life of a good Christian. I feel confident Granny Eve saw Halley's Comet as manna from Heaven. After stepping away from his reverie he'd wander down to the blue hole to see what shape the water was in. In a dry year, he'd likely find a thick covering of blue-green pond scum that only a frog-choking rain would clear out. In wintertime, he'd inspect the banks along the creek in search of bluebonnet sprouts so he could make a prediction about those precious blooms at the dinner table. Unless there was a death in the family, these trips never varied in the forty-plus years my grandparents lived on Hartland Avenue.

Before he left, he'd stop at the well and fill gallon jugs with well water to take back to Houston. My grandparents never adapted to the taste of city water, and Grandmother even washed her hair in the soft artesian water, a thing I found curious until I drilled my own water well decades later. Long after Granddad's death, I found out quite by happenstance just what a sacred commodity that well water actually was after my father handed me a box full of old photographs and letters. As I sorted through the box, reminiscing as I went, I discovered the draft of a letter that Granddad had written in pencil on Big Chief tablet paper in 1958. The subject is water, and there's no doubt in my mind that as he wrote it, he was thinking back to the case of typhoid fever he managed to survive in his youth, thanks in part to his good genes and an iron will.

It's a letter that I cherish to this day:

> Last year about the middle of summer I visited my farm. I happened down to my little Blue Branch (creek) and I noticed the water looked a nasty yellowish brown color instead of its old clear blue, color. I went up stream to seek the source of this color and odor. I found on Friemel's place some hogs in the Branch. I contacted Mr. Gus Friemel in Port Lavaca and this much of the trouble stopped. But this wasn't the real Source of the trouble. Inquiring further, I met a party telling me the real source was a pig Parlor on a concrete slab operated by Ruben Mass right on the Bank of Blue Branch about 10 ft. from the water. The head water or beginning of Blue Branch water flow is about 20 ft. above this concrete slab. So a few days later I called on Mr. Mass. I told him he was ruining me downstream with hog manure, maggots and stink, in other words converting the Blue Branch to an open sewer. The average flow of Blue Branch in summer flow is a stream, about all that can flow thru a 5 in. pipe; normal flow. Mr. Mass said he would do something about it; but it continued all last summer polluting the stream with maggots and hog manure as he would flush this manure off daily with a strong water hose into Blue Branch and normal flow of stream would bring this putrid mess down on my farm, manure and maggots in the flow of water.
>
> About the first week in July, 1959 this year, Mr. M.A. Roberts (a Highway Engineer) living in my farm home sent me word that the water in the well stunk and tasted bad. So he had the well thoroughly cleaned costing $25.00 for the job. Mr. Roberts, about 3 days later, sent a sample of the well water to Austin; the sample came back

saying that coliform organisms present after flushing the well good for about 5 days. I sent a sample to Austin Texas, the report was the same: Pollution. Mr. Roberts checked Mr. Mass's pig Parlor and so did I, Mr. Mass was with us and we both found that although Mr. Mass had stopped putting hog manure in the creek he was spraying or fogging water on a concrete slab for hogs to wallow in, then water runs into the creek and on down on me, thus polluting stream. My well is located about 500 yds. straight downstream from the pig Parlor.

The bottom of my well is about 3 feet lower than the bed of creek. It is a dug well that has been there about 120 years and has never had any trouble. This hog situation caused me to have to abandon present well and have Mr. George Housemann to drill me another costing $1000.00 more or less by a few dollars. Had Mr. Mass believed in the Golden Rule this would never have happened. I care not what Mr. Mass does or raises on his place, whether he raises 1 hog or 1000 hogs as long as he keeps everything that originated putrid on his place, keep it on his place and not run it down on me. He has placed himself liable for a law suit, by doing so.

Mr. Ed. Bardin is my cousin and neighbor to Mr. Mass. Let's say Mr. Bardin would sell his place, and I would buy it. The elevation would then put me above Mr. Mass. How would he like for me to build a pig parlor and run this refuse right by Mr. Mass's house and then on down to his well? The shoe would be on the other foot then. Remember the Golden Rule. How would he like it? The only way Mr. Mass can show that he is in real earnest to stop pollution is that you suggest to him to move his concrete hog parlor from its present location on *the creek bank to up to within a few feet of his barn on the back side of his place where none of the sewerage can get to Blue Branch. If Mr. Mass refuses to do this I will have to bring a law suit against him asking $1000.00 cost of my new well (plus) $2000.00 damage to value of my property and cost of attorney fees. Totaling $3000.00 + In the event I would lose the suit it would still cost him about $1000.00 to defend himself in court. In the event I would win it would cost him about $4000.00? In the event he couldn't pay, we would have to garnishee his pay check.*

If Mr. Mass will move his hog parlor as outlined above, I will not sue. I will drop the whole thing. This pollution could cause sickness or death to my children or grandchildren playing in or around said stream of water or Mr. Roberts' cattle, his family or anyone else that would come in contact with said stream of water. Mr. Mass has 3 neighbors that don't like the situation but won't do anything about it. They don't like the stink or flies. My problem is that of pollution that is costing me. When a person sends down pollution on a neighbor downstream, he is playing so near the border line of serious trouble, sickness and death for the entire family and livestock. This friendship may be lost for the rest of their lives; or a big expensive ugly law suit where somebody gets hurt bad financially. Is it worth it? A person is playing with double trouble. Think. When a man pollutes a neighbor he places himself liable. By not polluting a neighbor you escape all this. You both sleep well at night and stay friends. Choose. The way I see it is if a man has got to have a pig parlor and raise hogs, buy himself a 50 or 100-acre

Sitting a few yards behind the old kitchen, the abandoned water well resembles a weed-covered buffalo hump, the hole filled in long ago with dirt, rocks, and bric-a-brac to keep children from falling in. One of my father's chores as a shirt-tail kid, a chore he always dreaded, was cleaning the walls of the well, Granddad lowering him slowly in a wooden bucket as he wiped off spider webs and dust from the sides with a brush until he reached the bottom; that was a dark, creepy, confined space he was glad to get out of. I don't have the timeline for it, but the new house was equipped with indoor plumbing to the bathroom and indoor kitchen, so a cistern was added and a new chore arose, one that he shared with his brothers, pumping the cistern to full capacity to keep the water pressure up inside the house.

My father never had any horror stories about surviving the Great Depression. Their dairy farm was more or less self-sufficient. A verdant vegetable garden and a fruit orchard adjacent to the house thrived with a little help from composted manure, irrigating with well water when rain was scarce. Both have been kept up and replanted many times over, a mainstay for well over a century. Reading it reminded me of the trips he and Granny took in retirement. In 1961, having recovered from his trepidations about Alaska's statehood, my grandparents decided to explore a bit of new country themselves, driving their Comet station wagon to Anchorage, Alaska, where they took in the snowcapped mountains surrounding Lake Louise before heading to Fairbanks, driving a portion of the AL-CAN highway and camping in a baker's tent along the way. For their golden wedding anniversary in 1966, Granddad booked a cruise to the Bahamas on the good ship Ariadne. And on their fifty-fifth, they flew to Hawaii, their first time in the air, Granny nervous as a cat as they cruised high above the blue waters of the Pacific.

But nothing made Granddad's heart swell like his "little girl" or his little Blue Branch. After Granny died, he said he'd lost his right arm. They'd waltzed across Texas for seventy years. He did hang on just long enough to see Halley's Comet come round again before he passed away in 1986 at the age of eighty-nine. ⚘

My grandparents, Elsie and Ivan, 1975. (Houston Chronicle Archives)

Chapter 5 – The Sue-Ben

A weather-beaten cabin cruiser sitting on the grounds of a land-locked Texas ranch might seem as unlikely a sight to a passerby as spotting an igloo in the middle of Death Valley. After my father parked the *Sue-Ben* under an oak tree behind the old corral, threw a tarp over the hull and walked away twenty years ago, the boat was no better off than an old junked car that's been dumped somewhere out of sight and out of mind. I had hoped that eventually he'd give the boat a better resting place, one protected from the elements, but after he replaced our first family boat with a new Grady White, the *Sue-Ben* fell into a state of neglect.

While the boat sits in a dry-dock of Spanish moss, acorns, fallen leaves, and ant mounds, during visits to the ranch I'll stop on my way to the blue hole, lifting the mangy old tarp to inspect the hull, remembering the carefree days I spent with my family sitting on its decks and coasting across the emerald green waters of the Gulf. How many more layers of paint have eroded away since the last time I looked? And how many layers of memory will surface as I inspect another patch of dry rot? It took my father the better part of a year to build the *Sue-Ben*, a cabin cruiser that began as a dream, and later, a plan Dad ordered from *Popular Mechanics* magazine. The day he announced his decision to build it, he may as well have said we were sailing off to Borneo in a homemade raft. I was ten at the time, and though Dad was a skilled carpenter, boat-building sounded like a project best left to the experts.

That we weren't going to spring for a ready-made boat came as no surprise. Aside from the fact that Dad loved a good challenge, we always lived within our means. An engineer and tireless tinker, he'd already built a sunroom across the back of our house in Houston, later turning the front porch into a bedroom for my brother. We'd grown accustomed to the smell of sawdust, but it was hard to imagine that the end result of a stack of plywood, marine caulk, and stainless-steel screws might someday materialize into a cabin cruiser—and a *seaworthy* one at that.

The year was 1956. And for the better part of that year, an inner frenzy kept Dad working late into the night, the constant whir of his table saw our raucous lullaby. On a bad day he'd bust a thumb, or a part he was expecting hadn't shown up, or something didn't fit just right. But if he walked through the house whistling the "Toreador Song" from *Carmen*, we knew things were going well. That was the thing about my dad; he wasn't the stereotypical Texan. Oh, he was a *proud* Texan, to be sure, but he appreciated the classics along with good literature. It wasn't surprising to find a Strauss waltz on the turntable or a Somerset Maugham on his bedside table, not uncommon for him to quote a line from Shakespeare or Sir Walter Scott. Mother called him Ivanhoe, her pet name, always given with affection.

Dad was never satisfied unless he was making something with his own hands. I never knew a time when he didn't have projects, some that never saw fruition, like the summer he seemed determined to build a window unit air conditioner to save money. I recall Mother sticking her head inside the garage door with one last desperate plea, "Ivan, can't we just *buy* an air conditioner like the neighbors?"

But during that year of boat-building, our one-car garage morphed into the nerve center of our Riley Street home, news of the construction moving from house to house with the speed of a drag racer carrying a megaphone. I think our friends were equally as enthralled and curious about the whole aspect of boat-building. Mr. Miles, a white-haired retiree who lived next door, popped his head inside the garage on a regular basis. After the hull came together, some of the other men-folk were more than happy to help Dad move it onto sawhorses in the driveway.

For us, that year of boatbuilding dragged by like wet sand through an hourglass. It was all mother could do to pry Dad away from the garage long enough to eat. Even though we saw some progress being made, on the days we badgered him about a completion date, he showed the patience of Job, responding with the kind of wit that satisfies children: "You know what the monkey said when he got his tail caught in the lawnmower?" he'd smile. "It won't be long now."

When at last the *Sue-Ben* was born in the spring of 1957, measuring 18 feet from fore to aft, green and white pinstripes running along the waterline of its white hull, we learned that clear-cut goals are attainable. Neighbors filed past admiring the canvas decks and running lights and Mr. Miles climbed inside the mahogany cabin, testing the sliding Plexiglas windows.

After Dad checked the want ads and found a slightly used Johnson outboard motor and trailer, we drove to Clear Lake in the wee hours of a Saturday morning—so early, in fact, my mother mistook a refinery flare shrouded in fog for the rising sun. We had a good laugh from the back seat of our green Plymouth sedan, and mother christened the boat with a bottle of cheap champagne wrapped in a towel before Dad backed the trailer down the launch with me riding shotgun.

The *Sue-Ben*, named for me and my brother, proved quite seaworthy, and on her maiden voyage at Clear Lake, I felt like a princess taking a spin on the royal yacht. In the beginning, we didn't venture too far from shore, but over time explored the larger waters of Galveston Bay, learning how to navigate with maps and landmarks. We always carried an ice chest full of Jax beer and Cokes, and sometimes we'd drop anchor near a deserted stretch of beach and wade ashore, holding the picnic basket of salami sandwiches overhead while dodging jelly fish.

On a later trip in the Gulf, we lost sight of land for the first time, drifting aimlessly and casting our lines in water too deep to set anchor. We hadn't seen another boat in hours, and though we knew Dad wouldn't deliberately put us in harm's way, neither were we in the parking lot of a shopping mall. While he plotted our course back, using nautical maps and a compass, Mom gave him one of her scalding, what-have-you-gotten-us-into looks, retreating to the cabin to smoke a cigarette and stare out the cabin window. He reassured her in his casual way that we'd find the launch, then chuckled, "There's plenty of flares on board," which produced an even dimmer go-to-hell smile from Mom.

We spent most every Saturday fishing and snorkeling near abandoned offshore rigs in the Gulf, living our version of the American Dream. We quickly learned the thrill of that first catch along with the disappointment of the big one that got away. One day I'd fought and reeled in a sizeable ling on sore arms, Dad dipping the net into the water right before the line snapped—a real heartbreaker. We learned about sea legs, sunburn chills and that rocking sensation in bed at night, the body's reaction to a pleasant day riding the swells. We also learned considerable respect for the biting sting of a Portuguese man-of-war and the awesome fury of a squall, a high-seas hell-broth we managed to outrun on several occasions.

The day Dad let me take over the helm marked a milestone in my life more significant than my first date or my first time behind the wheel of the family car. I opened the throttle with feverish intent, the *Sue-Ben* launching across the water like a rocket. Dad held on for dear life, clutching his Amoco hat and laughing all the way. Along with the fun came responsibilities. Back at the house, we treated the boat with meticulous care, washing it down after every saltwater trip, polishing the *Sue-Ben* like the family jewel she had become.

During our college years, we spent less and less time on the boat, and Dad and his lifelong friend and fishing buddy, Robert Pieratt, decided to rig it up for shrimping. Robert and Dad grew up together in La Grange, inseparable until World War II broke out and they rallied to the cause. Houston was booming after the war, and a lot of Dad's friends settled there, many with foreign wives. It wasn't unusual to hear an English or Scottish accent in the crowd, and after Robert settled in Giddings with his German bride, we grew accustomed to Mary Lou's accent as well. Giddings is another lazy Texas town down the road from LaGrange, and when Robert finished his route driving a Jax Beer truck, we'd stop in and play with his kids, or meet them at Lake Bastrop for a picnic.

Robert was a pleasure to be around, full of laughter, one of those people who wake up on the right side of the bed every day. It wasn't long before he moved his family to Houston, bought a house not far from ours, enrolled in law school, passed the bar, and hung out his shingle. Although he was a successful defense attorney, Robert helped me with my divorce and other legal matters, making me feel whole again as he put a positive spin on any given situation in his light-hearted way.

Robert was enthused about the prospects of shrimping, phoning the house regularly to see how Dad was progressing with the mast. As soon as Dad fastened the first Texas Bay Shrimp license plate to his trailer, he and Robert located a man who made trawling nets special-order. Robert enjoyed reliving the day they drove across town to pick it up, shocked when they discovered the net-maker was blind. They didn't realize this until he dropped a tool on the floor of his shop, and, stooping down to get it, grabbed Dad's foot instead.

For more years than I can remember, at least until the Vietnamese moved in and competed with the shrimping industry, Dad and Robert kept family and friends well stocked with fresh Gulf shrimp, and Mom collected enough recipes to rival Forrest Gump. Robert was crazy about Mom's gumbo, a recipe I've only recently mastered by hook and by crook, remembering she always added a dash of Kitchen Bouquet at the end.

Their stories spun in endless circles around the supper table. There was the day Dad and Robert had a flat tire on the way to the coast and pulled into the parking lot of a funeral home, only to get caught in the middle of a funeral procession while trying to change the flat. Or the time the mast wouldn't clear the railroad swing bridge across Galveston Bay. Signaling the bridge operator to open up with a few blasts from their portable fog horn, they made it to the other side only to find the water too choppy. Turning back right after the bridge closed, they blew the horn again. The bridge-keeper obliged them, but hung out of his booth in a fist-shaking tirade for the inconvenience of one small boat. I can still picture Dad and Robert feeding off each another with gales of laughter as they passed through to calmer waters, another story to tell on down the road.

Eventually, Robert turned over his Houston practice to his son and relocated to Brenham, where he won a judgeship. After he retired from the bench, he and Mary Lou moved back to Houston and spent weekends at their country place outside of Brenham. I drove over there with Dad only once. Robert had stocked his pond with cat fish and couldn't wait to show me how he'd trained them to respond to his car horn to get fed.

Robert paid me the highest compliment anyone could when he asked for a copy of the eulogy I'd written for my grandfather. The last time I saw Robert was at my mother's funeral. He was wearing his trademark blue seersucker suit and walked up to me after the service. "You like it up there in North Carolina," he'd smiled. "I trained as a pilot up there while I was in the service. It's nice country." When I inquired about Mary Lou, he said she couldn't make it. "She's been sick ever since we got back from that trip to India. You sure have to watch what you eat over in that part of the world," he laughed.

One night many years later, Mary Lou made a frantic phone call to Dad, saying that Robert was in some kind of trouble, that he'd phoned her from Houston and sounded confused about where he was. That he'd said he was waiting for her at a bus stop. Could Dad go check on his whereabouts until she could get to town? Dad found his friend on a familiar street corner in front of a bar they'd frequented through the years, managing to bundle him into his car and get him back to their house before calling the paramedics.

Robert had suffered a debilitating stroke that left him with stroke-related Alzheimer's. He lived out his days strapped to a wheelchair in an acute care facility, unable to raise his head, living among strangers, not recognizing the three children he adored. But Alzheimer's is a strange disease. Whenever Dad dropped by to see him, Robert somehow recognized his old friend, and he'd shout, loud enough for all to hear, "Hey Ivan! Are we on the boat, Ivan?" Sometimes he'd ramble, his words incoherent to all but my father, about being on the boat again, describing the Sue-Ben or some fishing trip from long ago before retreating into the darkness that had taken over his life.

We were at the Blue Branch the day Dad got a phone call from Houston that Robert had passed away. There'd be no funeral service and his ashes would be scattered later on. Dad took the news as well as can be expected, though it may have explained the night terror he'd suffered the night before, rousting me from my bunk at three a.m. The next morning when I questioned him about his nightmare, he said he couldn't recall anything about it. I'll never forget his bloodcurdling screams that night or how helpless I felt. The *Sue-Ben* is more than just a deserted boat rotting on a Texas ranch. It's a time capsule of those salad days when Dad and Robert hadn't a care in the world, a symbol of unbridled spirit and friendship. I've long since forgotten how to tie a half hitch or a bowline knot, but I can still see my mother sitting inside that cabin puffing away on a Kent. I remember mornings rolling out of bed at 3 a.m., the smell of coffee poured from a Thermos, and eating sweet rolls from the Rainbow Bakery. I remember the time we forgot the picnic basket and Dad saved the day, stepping out of the cabin carrying a can of sardines and crackers on a tray, a napkin draped across his arm like a waiter on a cruise ship.

I can still feel the rush of chasing a school of flying fish skimming over the waters ahead and the sticky salt air on my skin. I remember long evenings sitting under a task lamp, heading shrimp with my brother in the garage, Mother peeking through the door in hopes there weren't too many more, Dad humoring Mom, "Don't worry, Josephine." And after more years have passed than I care to think about, I can still hear the laughter. 🪶

The Sue-Ben's maiden voyage at Clear Lake, Texas (Author on top deck)

Chapter 6 – No Funeral!

Quiet lies the body under the limb…
The ground's a harp strung with shadows.

— MIDDLE CREEK POEMS, BY SHELBY STEPHENSON

After most of our Houston neighbors had fled to area shelters, I rode out my first hurricane, Hurricane Carla, with my parents in September of 1961. In August of 1983, I sat through Alicia all alone in my modest Houston rental and swore I'd never do it again. When Hurricane Fran slam-dunked the North Carolina coast in September of 1996, my husband and I slept in the basement of our new house in Johnston County as the eye tracked up Interstate 40, two miles away as the crow flies, rattling our garage doors until I thought they'd fly off their hinges. Later that same week my brother called from the ranch. I assumed he wanted to know how we'd weathered the storm. We'd done a lot to prepare for Fran, but I was ill-prepared for his news: My mother had just suffered a fatal heart attack.

As I phoned Kerry in Wilmington, I felt as though I was in the eye of Fran all over again. Kerry and my mother had been kindred spirits, and I dreaded telling him that his Grammer had passed away. When his girlfriend said he'd gone to the Outer Banks to surf for the weekend, I panicked. It's a five-hour drive, plus a ferryboat ride from our house to Cape Hatteras. How on earth would we find him? She put the word out to friends, and several agonizing hours later, a park ranger found him at the Bodie Island Light House and made the notification. He was inconsolable.

Mother had said all through the years that when her time came, she did *not* want a funeral. She'd almost scream the words, "No funeral!" I never asked why. Whether the funerals she attended in childhood had had a bad effect on her, or she found funerals in general too depressing, I never questioned. But funerals are really for the living, and we started making preparations.

During our drive from the airport, I was almost relieved when Dad turned all the arrangements over to me. It was something else to focus on. But as I picked through Mom's closet looking for the last dress she'd ever wear, I couldn't erase the image of her collapsing onto the bed at the cabin only twenty-four hours before. After careful consideration, I decided on the turquoise chiffon dress she'd worn when Dan and I married. A Rhode Island transplant, Mom got a kick out of Dan's Southern accent. Whenever she phoned the house she'd mimic him in fun and say, "It's yo momma." In lieu of a church wedding, we'd had one of those outdoor, weekend affairs on the San Marcos River. Mom had the time of her life. It seemed like a hundred years ago.

As I sorted through old photographs to use at the service, I thought about the bedtime prayer we said together every night, "Now I lay me down to sleep. I pray the Lord my soul to keep. If I should die before I wake. I pray the Lord my soul to take." I thought about the carefree days of my childhood, singing songs from the "Hit Parade." At the age of five, I'd already mapped out my professional career as a singer, and spent many happy hours practicing my routines on the front porch. Mom would coach me and sometimes we'd sing together. She had a rich, earthy voice, and could have given Ella Fitzgerald a run for her money with her rendition of "Bewitched, Bothered and Bewildered."

I decided to take my parents' engagement picture for the remembrance table. Dad's wearing his khaki Air Force uniform, and I still feel lucky that Mom passed her Colgate smile on to me. Theirs is the quintessential love story, and I never tired of hearing Mom relive their chance meeting during a weekend furlough as World War II was ending.

It seemed that in his letters home, Uncle Ben, my mom's brother, spoke highly of his new friend, Tex. Soon after, Mother and Gram Follett caught a train from New York to meet him.

After a whirlwind courtship through the mail, Mom broke off her engagement to Howie and eloped with Tex. After her plans for a big church wedding backfired, my grandmother went into such a tailspin that she disowned my mother. On April 14, 1944, my folks were married in a small ceremony in La Junta, Colorado where my dad was stationed at that time.

Mom loved to say she'd left the smallest state to live in the biggest. After his discharge, they lived with my grandparents in Houston until Dad could find work. His first job offer was to manage a cattle ranch in west Texas for a family friend, the ranch being somewhere west of Alpine and east of Big Bend. But my mother's romantic image of ranch life came to an abrupt halt as they pulled up to the gate in the middle of the night. As soon as she heard the high lonesome sound of the coyotes, yipping and howling from all directions, she wanted no part of the ranching community, so unnerved that Dad couldn't coax her out of the car. They back-tracked to Alpine, found a motel, and drove back to Houston the next morning. Edna Ferber would have had a field day with the material, but wrote *Giant* instead.

The next morning, we drove to the Blue Branch to prepare for my mother's service. From the outside looking in, you'd have thought all of the men-folk had gone a little bit haywire. But we'd done so much crying over the telephone that I suppose we were all cried out. Dad spent every waking moment on his riding mower, and while my husband swept clippings from the sidewalks around the house, my brother set up some bottles and cans for target practice in the corral. I hadn't seen Kerry all day.

I was on the phone with the funeral director composing Mom's obituary for the paper, jumping with each *Bam! Bam!* of Ben's .44 magnum. When she asked for the year Mom was born, my mind went blank. I rang the plantation bell outside to summon Dad, remembering the day he bought it at a flea market in North Carolina. He put it high up on a pole at a corner of the cabin, and Mother would yank the rope at mealtime or whenever one of us had a phone call. The list of details seemed endless, and with the barrage of incoming calls and outgoing calls, and the gunfire, I hung up late in the day feeling like an exposed nerve.

Yellow roses had always been Mom's favorite flower, so I drove into La Grange, two miles as the crow flies from the ranch, to order a casket spray. When the florist said there'd been a run on yellow roses that weekend, my mind, in its delirium, flashed back to the Rose Ball my junior year at Sam Houston State. It was customary for your beau to send a dozen long-stemmed red roses on the day of the ball, and I'd been waiting patiently in my dorm room for the delivery. When my long white floral box finally arrived, I ripped it open only to find a dozen plastic dime store roses with an apologetic note. I'd been shattered to learn there'd been a run on roses that day as well. Mom used to say that life is full of little disappointments, so I improvised and took the dozen yellow roses they had for the remembrance table, ordered a spray of daisies, and left for the funeral home.

Savage Funeral Home is a low-slung building of dun-colored brick just down the street from the florist and Stoltz Memorials, conveniently located across the street from City Cemetery. As I crossed the tracks that run through the east part of town and pulled under the portico, a young dark-haired woman on a riding mower, the wife of the funeral director, Mrs. Savage as it turned out, came over to greet me, escorting me through a side entrance.

I don't consider myself a snob about such things, and I don't know what I expected to find in a small Texas town of 2,000 people. Certainly not the crystal chandeliers or the velvet upholstery and other plush underpinnings of an Earthman's or a Settegast-Kopf, the two funeral homes in Houston I was familiar with. But as funeral homes go, it was a stark, no-frills kind of place that wasn't to my liking.

I thought about the Episcopal Church in the center of town with its exquisite stained glass windows and elegant appointments, but my parents dropped out of the church scene after I left for college, so there wasn't much to be done about it. In the absence of any gilt-framed watercolors of serene landscapes, the two floral arrangements that had arrived earlier in the day helped soften an otherwise barren room of linoleum flooring and folding chairs.

I hoped the wave of apprehension washing over me didn't show as I read the attached cards, one from Mom's brother Ben, who'd suffered a stroke some years back, the other from my dear friend Billy, sending his regrets from an oil rig off the Louisiana coast. The attractive and pleasant Mrs. Savage handed me a tri-fold brochure of musical selections, all categorized: Classical, Pops and Easy Instrumentals, all neatly numbered like the songs on a juke box. I scanned the list, unable to make any decision.

I had Mother's chiffon dress, still on a hanger in a dry cleaning bag, slung over one arm. After I handed Mrs. Savage the pearl earbobs Mom was never without, along with her eyeglasses, the oversized plastic frames of pink tortoiseshell, she said my mother would be ready for viewing sometime that afternoon. "She wears her hair pulled back in a bun at the nape of her neck," I said, trying to distance myself from the image of my mother lying prone on a stainless steel table in the back room of a strange and inglorious place, and left in a state of melancholy.

"Always" had been a popular song when my parents wed. It was *their* song, the song played at their elopement in a wedding chapel in La Junta, Colorado. Over lunch with Dad, I suggested it as a possible music selection, but he shook his head, saying it would just do him in to hear it. I didn't understand him at first, but my mother's voice interceded with, "Don't push it, Susan!" He also didn't want any part of "In the Sweet By and By," or any other sad old church hymns. Everyone handles grief in their own way, and I respected his wishes. He picked two songs that were popular during their courtship in New England, and I phoned the funeral director with his choices: "Moonlight in Vermont" and "Canadian Sunset." Later in the day, he added "Moon River," a song Mom liked from the 1960s.

I finally spotted Kerry wandering around outside like a lost soul. He'd been stewing all day about not getting the chance to say goodbye to Mom. As a rule, Perry men don't cry. But he's the most like my mother, a sensitive kid whose tears come easily. I consoled him as best I could in the slanting shadows of the barn.

On the evening before the service things weren't shaping up the way I'd hoped. My husband had to return to North Carolina on unexpected business and we hadn't heard anything from Dad's cousin Jack, a retired Methodist minister in San Antonio. Since Jack was supposed to conduct the service, Dad called to check on him. His wife, Trudy, answered and said he'd been rushed to the hospital for emergency surgery. After Dad hung up, all eyes were on me to handle the service.

Cousin Jack. Oh, how I'd miss him. His ministry had been way out west, in Utopia, Texas, or, as Jack put it, "from cain't see to cain't see." In his post-Christmas newsletter he wrote that Trudy was on a diet of "wind soup and air pudding," and that he'd just gotten over the shotgun flu. Just when you think you've recovered, it hits you with the other barrel.

I was beginning to have serious doubts about our funeral plans when the funeral director called and put me in touch with Ann Hoey, an Episcopal minister in La Grange. Reverend Hoey agreed to lead the service, so I carried Dad's portable typewriter to the porch of the cabin to write Mom's eulogy.

It isn't always easy being the family scribe, and I've never been able to write under pressure. In my grief-ridden state, the words just weren't coming. To make matters worse, the key for the letter "K" kept sticking. I couldn't believe how many times I needed the letter "K," quitting in bitter frustration at half a page. It wasn't until Uncle Ben called from Vermont and said they'd held their own service for her up there that something inside began to click. As he spoke of her Christian name, Josephine Isabella, I started getting un-stuck. He explained that Isabella was her grandmother's name, and after I hung up, the eulogy started showing more promise. I worked until bedtime, writing about her name.

Dad snored from pure exhaustion in the next room, but I couldn't sleep. At two in the morning, and dog tired, I was still thinking about the service. I was going over my lame eulogy for the umpteenth time when one resonating *Gonnnnngggggg* split the night like thunder, rolling across the yard to the pond and through the distant woods. I shot up from my bunk and ran to the window, trying to rationalize what I'd heard while Dad, seemingly in a coma, never stirred. In the blue shadows of the vapor lamp, I couldn't see a thing that gave me a clue about the mystery bell-ring. Not even our horse, Sugar, could have managed it. Apparently I was the only one who heard it, and I lay in a pool of irrational thought until morning.

We met with Reverend Hoey before the service and she put me right at ease. She looked like an angel in her a flowing white robe. Assuming she'd deliver the eulogy, I handed her my draft, surprised when she handed it back and said that I should deliver it, that she'd come to my rescue if I broke down. I'd marked some passages in one of Mom's favorite books, but she nixed the idea. The reverend found *Evangeline* much too depressing, and said the service was to be a *celebration* of my mother's life. I could hardly get my mind around the word "celebration," much less how I'd turn this thing around with all of us feeling so low, leaving the room thinking my eulogy needed a major rewrite.

Dad and I huddled together in the front row. As "Moon River," "Canadian Sunset," and "Moonlight in Vermont" played for the third time, Dad complained that he could barely hear the music. "All the songs sound alike," he whispered. In truth, the songs sounded much too funereal and maudlin for my taste. I was thinking they couldn't have messed up "Moon River" any more if they'd tried when Dad rolled his eyes and whispered, "We forgot to call Richard Rain." Oh my Lord! Mom's half-brother in Florida. I felt two inches tall. The words "no funeral" ran through my head like a clap of thunder.

When the reverend gave me the nod, I stood at the podium and stumbled nervously over my words, thinking I hadn't said all the things I'd really meant to say about Mom. How she'd laughed at all my feeble jokes. How proud she'd been of my every accomplishment, no matter how mundane. How she'd devoted her life to us, clairvoyant with regard to her family. I wasn't going to bring up her nervous breakdown and subsequent clinical depression and all the years we somehow kept it together as a family. Everybody knew about it. Why hash over it? This was supposed to be a *celebration* of her life. But underneath all her emotional baggage, her struggle with clinical depression, I forgot to say what a boundless sense of humor she had. How she'd joke that all of her shrinks had been Irish, from Dr. Finney to Dr. Molloy to Dr. Ryan. And I didn't even get everything about her name right. I'd forgotten to say that her father called her Jif, a nickname using her initials, and that close friends and family called her Joey, or Joe for short. Since she lived so many years in dysfunction, in death I wanted perfection, and I felt that I'd missed the mark.

Nearing the end of my delivery, I remembered how Mom always answered my childhood complaints with, "I'm doing the best I can, Susan." I took those words to heart. Somehow I'd gotten through my mother's eulogy, and under the circumstances, I'd done the best I could.

After the service, family and friends gathered back at the ranch carrying casseroles. While car doors slammed outside, people filed into the house with high praise for my eulogy. Then the phone rang: It was a family friend, Connie, who said she couldn't make it with the honey-baked ham she'd promised. Despite all the covered dishes on the table, we had no meat course. I don't know why a little thing like a *ham* made me feel so defeated, but it did, and when the walls started closing in on me, I left the house.

Reverend Hoey joined me in the shade of the Perry Oak, admiring its enormous trunk and sprawling limbs that dwarf the house. A dark-eyed brunette with a warm smile, she reminded me of my mother in middle age. She asked me the name of the ranch. Blue Branch Ranch can be quite the tongue-twister, and we giggled as she tried repeating it a few times real fast. It was the first time I'd laughed in days, and as we lingered at the edge of the yard, I caught myself wondering if she was single. With her dark eyes and hair, she reminded of my mother at age fifty. She certainly had my mother's wit and might make a good companion for Daddy.

The next morning the pasture came alive with painted lady butterflies. They seemed to be everywhere, delicate and full of life, fluttering from pasture to fence to yard, collecting dew from every blade of grass. As I watched them, I heard my mother's voice whisper "Pretty." Pretty was my first word, and as I watched them spiral up to the heavens, I felt for the first time that her spirit had finally been set free. It was a beautiful sight.

I stayed an extra week to help my father cope and to tend to the usual paperwork involved with someone's passing. When I retired to my old bedroom each night, I'd sink into a reverie as I gazed at Mom and Dad's engagement picture on the dresser. Mom had a radiant smile and her teeth reminded me of a perfect set of Mikimoto pearls. But a condition called dry mouth brought on by her medications caused her to lose them. She never got used to her dentures, refusing to wear them unless I begged her. The doctor said that years of chain smoking led to her congestive heart failure. She could hardly put one foot in front of the other toward the end. "So I live six more months," she'd respond when my father kept telling her that she couldn't live on Cokes and cigarettes alone, that she wasn't nineteen any more. It hardly seemed fair that after a lifetime of getting her head together, her body fell apart. Ten years after her death, the FDA pulled Mellaril, an antidepressant Mom had taken most of her adult life, from the market after studies found it caused severe cardiac arrhythmias, a sobering discovery.

After returning to North Carolina, I was still having trouble saying goodbye. Yellow has never been a color I gravitate to, but I couldn't seem to get enough of it in my life, filling our deck with yellow mums and every blooming thing I could find in yellow. I put together a memory box with some of her things: a small address book with a tapestry cover, Mom's pill box, her abalone lighter, my childhood prayer book, my letters to Santa, and a blue Bakelite pin that spelled *Josephine*. I wrapped up her black cloth gloves and my white baby shoes in tissue paper and tucked the box away on a shelf.

I hadn't been back long when another tropical depression popped up in the Gulf of Mexico and I thought, *Here we go again*. As the storm grew, I kept up with its progress from day to day. I could hardly believe it when The Weather Channel announced that Tropical Storm *Josephine* posed a threat from the Gulf Coast to the Carolinas. As storms go, Josephine never made it to the major leagues. She wobbled indecisively for days before she made landfall. I followed her every move as she danced up the east coast, caused some minor flooding in the Carolinas, and swirled past the Bodie Island Lighthouse. As Josephine began to stall out on the New England shore, I dug through my vintage record albums and put *Breakfast at Tiffany's* on the turntable. I wanted to hear "Moon River" again the way it should be heard, scratches and all. ⚘

Mom and Dad's engagement, 1944 (Joey and Ivan)

Chapter 7 – Letters Found

I walked away from the plot she sure-god
Did not prepare for anything she'd plant,
Her memory leaving her so she could
Not get up herself, flat in Sunnybrook…

— OUR WORLD BY SHELBY STEPHENSON

In the 1950s, long before PCs became common as popcorn, my mother began acting irrational, out of character. Besides tiring easily and going to bed right after the supper dishes were done, sometimes she'd walk about the house with her fingers in her ears trying to stop the voices. This strange behavior did quite a number on my psyche. I had my problems sleeping some nights, wondering what else might be in store. Since there were no websites enlightening the world about clinical depression—no Betty Ford Clinic or Tipper Gore appearances on *Oprah*—we dealt with it as best we could.

Dad hired a maid to help out with the ironing, and the one day a week that Ada ironed and watched soap operas, my baby brother and I accompanied our mother to Dr. Finney's office in downtown Houston for B-12 shots to boost her energy level. I didn't know much about psychiatrists at the time, but the nurses were always very friendly during our visits and gave us lollipops before we left.

Signs of her illness surfaced slowly. Most mornings before I got out of bed I'd overhear her belittling my father in one-sided arguments before he left for work. Then she missed my Christmas recital at school, stopped going to church, and lapsed into crying spells for no apparent reason. We were no angels, but sometimes she'd get out of control over small things, spanking us within an inch of our lives with one of Dad's leather belts.

Prior to these episodes, we'd had a tragedy in the family. Dad's brother, my beloved uncle Lelldon, died in a car wreck while working for an oil company in Iraq. We got the news just minutes after returning home from a going-away party for his wife, Aunt Laura, and my five cousins, who were to board a plane the next morning and join him in Baghdad for three years. There'd even been a write-up in the local paper about it. We're a close-knit family, and I'd never known or felt such heartache. The timing made his death doubly hard to take; my grandmother was inconsolable. It was the first time I'd seen my father cry. And Mom cried deep, heaving sobs all the night long.

But after all the grieving, she started obsessing about Dad's safety any time he left the house. Consequently, Dad passed up a number of promotions over the years because Mother didn't want him going out of town. I was eleven years old when Mom had her first nervous breakdown, going into a manic rage one evening and screaming like a mad woman before heaving a large cast-iron skillet at my father. It just missed his head and split in two when it hit the floor of the sunroom. I thought she was going to kill him. This episode ended with Dad wrestling Mom to the floor of the living room while Ben and I huddled together in the kitchen clutching our cat, Ginger. An ambulance whisked her away, and sometime later, while back at home, she tried to end her agony with an overdose of sleeping pills.

Just before school let out, in the early summer of 1958, Mom flew to Rhode Island to visit her family. She had to change planes in New York and ended up wandering the streets of the city, totally lost. She spent that summer in the mental ward of a hospital in Providence. While the state of Texas was experiencing a severe drought, the weather forecast for the Perry household called for gray skies followed by thunderstorms of epic proportions. With nothing to go on in regard to my mother's illness, I could only picture her in the starring role of the movie *Snake Pit*. Camping trips with my Girl Scout Troop offered an escape, but I had no friends to confide in. Children can be cruel, and I overheard hushed conversations about my "crazy mother" more than once. As I lay in bed at night, I longed to have my mother back—the normal one who comforted me when I skinned a knee, the mother who stood up for me and shouted *"I sway-uh"* (I swear) in her Rhode Island accent after Mrs. Miles accused me of raiding her vegetable patch, the one who scolded my father good— naturedly whenever he let us have a sip of his beer, or "beeyuh."

My father was deeply devoted to Mom, stoic throughout that tumultuous summer. A weaker man would have bailed out, but I remember many nights passing their bedroom door and seeing him kneeling in prayer at their bedside. While there's no substitute for mother-love, his bedtime stories were an escape to fantasyland each night, and he seemed to have an endless supply about his boyhood escapades at the Blue Branch, or his wild charades and mishaps in flight training during World War II.

We kept up with Mom's progress through letters, but I was in the dark for the most part, gleaning what I could through muffled phone conversations. I knew that her doctors had decided against a frontal lobotomy and that she was undergoing shock treatments, things I knew nothing about until 1975 when *One Flew Over the Cuckoo's Nest* hit theaters.

Mom's re-entry into society was a slow one. Unlike diseases such as polio, mental problems had a stigma attached, one that branded my family. Many of her friends deserted her at the lowest point in her life. It wasn't their fault; I'm sure they felt as helpless as we did. But I don't remember any outpourings of sympathy upon her return as when someone is diagnosed with cancer or suffers a broken bone. Texas was thirty-five years behind in mental health treatment, and group therapy hadn't reached our neck of the woods yet.

Mother seemed distant for a time, and I was horrified to discover that, due to the electroshock treatments, she'd lost part of her memory. I worried that she'd never get it back. Unbeknownst to me, Daddy had saved all the letters she'd written during her confinement at the Charles

V. Chapin Hospital. They're written in pencil on plain white paper, each letter folded and creased like an accordion. Having read them, I know more about her ordeal, and have a clearer picture of the hospital, a facility that didn't sound nearly as notorious and dark as the one portrayed in the *Cuckoo's Nest* movie.

Her letters home read like this: "June 13, 1958. Well I'm here …and I guess it's for the best…Hope I can leave in about three weeks. Take care of yourselves." – *Your Loving Wife*

On June 23, she wrote that she'd had two shock treatments and mentions a Doctor Goldstein, a Doctor Hughes, and a Doctor Lyte. There's a TV room with puzzles and games. There's a big yard, and "they take a walk every day or play softball." She wrote a letter to Granny Perry telling her how sorry she was for all the things she said in anger and hoping she'll forgive her.

I unfold another. Each letter reminds me of a piece of origami, one folded precisely like the next. I learn that she kept a picture of us by her bed along with a card I sent, letters from Dad, and one from our neighbor Zelda. She had a nice view of Providence College across the street. A priest came by almost every night and they had a sing. She was eating well and weighed 120 pounds and needed money for cigarettes. She had to beg a few until my uncle Warren could bring her some. In the next letter, she'd had her third shock treatment and repeated the same information from her previous letters, about the TV room and the nice letter from Zelda and the card I sent. "You and the children are my whole life," she says, along with a P.S.: "I wish you'd send me some money for cigarettes. I'm low."

I unfold another. Dr. Hughes has told her that he never gives more than twenty shock treatments and she hopes she won't need more than five. My grandmother Follett has brought her a box of chocolates and they're all enjoying them. Another patient, a Mrs. Hubbard, got to go home after only five shock treatments. Mom helps out in the kitchen and keeps busy drying dishes. She feels lost at times and looks forward to the day she'll return to her own house. She looks at our picture every night before bed and says a prayer. She makes a reference to Dad's letter about me baking a spice cake, noting that I'll make a lovely wife and mother someday, and signed it *Your Loving Wife*.

(Dad was handy in the kitchen and at the grill. I remember him teaching me how to cut up a chicken one night for supper. I don't know why cutting up that chicken made me feel so special, but it did.)

I unfold another. She took another treatment and has lost track of how many, maybe five or six. She looks forward to the mail distribution every day and just got Dad's letter with some money he enclosed for cigarettes and incidentals. The hospital is nice, but she's anxious to see her honey and her Susan and her Ben and have a nice vacation before going back home to Texas, and signed it *Your Loving Wife*.

I unfold another. More origami. Mom's had about five shock treatments, she thinks. She's homesick and wants to come back to Houston and let Dr. Finney continue with her treatments. "Please write and tell me when you'll be traveling up here with the children. I miss you." As before, it's signed *Your Loving Wife*

Another letter reads, "July 9, 1958. Just woke up from another shock treatment. Providence College is right across the street from this hospital. One of the priests comes over almost every night and we have a nice sing. It sure lifts up my morale. When are you coming? Are you going to drive or fly? Please get me some Estee Lauder face powder and crème rouge blend. I'm very low on both. Ben and Elsie stopped by and brought me some clothes which sure will come in handy and they fit." – *Your Loving Wife*

I refold the last letter and put it back into a shoe box, remembering what rank amateurs we were regarding Mom's illness. Granny Perry meant well, but she thought two Anacin tablets could cure anything. In spite of that, she threw me a lifeline when I desperately needed one, picking me up for sleepovers and taking me shopping and sewing me pretty dresses. Even so, that summer felt like an eternity.

The first week of August, with a short hairdo compliments of Granny, and my new dresses neatly folded and packed in my suitcase, we left Houston for the four-day drive to Providence to pick up our precious cargo. Four days of flat tires and eating BLTs for lunch to save time even though Daddy, as a petroleum engineer, got a generous vacation; four days of driving sunup to sunset in our Plymouth Savoy, Daddy drafting behind big tractor-trailers as if on a racetrack, reading maps, taking a wrong turn, backtracking, and enduring some hazards along the way.

First mishap: the peaches we bought at a roadside stand in Georgia, so fuzzy they looked like a basket of giant cotton balls, the wind slicing through the window vents launching peach fuzz like summer snow as Dad motored on, my brother's skin erupting in hives, the tears flowing as he scratched his red whelps. Also etched in my mind is that day in the mountains of West Virginia. We'd just rounded a curve when a heavy wooden cart came careening down a steep hill, plowing through a split rail fence before crossing the road just up ahead and smashing into a tree. Daddy slammed on his brakes as we stared at the splintered cart in awe, feeling lucky to be alive. As he cleared debris from the road, a farmer came running down to lend a hand; he surmised that a cow had been rubbing against the cart, dislodging it in the process of scratching an itch.

When we weren't reading Burma Shave signs or counting the miles to the next Stuckey's, we slept. Periodically throughout each day, Daddy rousted us from deep slumber to take in points of interest. "Wake up kids. We're in Winston-Salem where they make all the cigarettes." We did some fun things, too. We stopped at the Smithsonian in D.C., where I took pictures of a dinosaur along with one of Charles Lindbergh's plane, the *Spirit of St. Louis,* with my Brownie Hawkeye box camera. Later on, we stopped in New York City where I took a picture of Dad and Ben standing in front of Macy's department store before we ate lunch at a place called an "automat," pulling sandwiches from glass doors that covered an entire wall. But the most exciting thing was boarding the elevator in the Empire State Building, knowing the longest elevator ride of my life was yet to come.

I don't know exactly how many shock treatments my mother endured, but in one of Uncle Warren's letters he indicated that in his discussion with Dr. Hughes, she'd had thirteen by mid-July, and the doctor felt that in her case twenty were advisable. He explained that at about the 17th to the 19th treatment, a change takes place in the patient, manifesting in several seemingly negative ways: the memory is extremely mixed up, the patient tends to be flip or fresh, and so on. These behaviors represent a treatment landmark, signaling that recovery will be complete in a matter of days. On a more practical matter, he indicated that Mom had about eight dollars left in her account, an adequate amount for cigarettes and other sundries.

We spent two weeks in Gram Follett's big barn of a house getting reacquainted with our mother, who seemed somewhat depleted after her ordeal. The weather was cool for August. "Indian summer," Gram said as she opened a picture album, pointing to a scene of my second birthday party on her front lawn. In the early days of our trips to Rhode Island, we took the train, just Mother, me, and Ben in a sleeper car. It was pure adventure for two shirttail kids. (Gram also took the train to visit us in Texas, though I don't know how she survived the summer heat!)

Gram's house sat atop a steep hill a block up from Narragansett Bay, where the summer air was rife with ocean smells as sailboats skimmed across the water and flotillas of swans bobbed like white corks near the shoreline. I saw my first horseshoe crab there, digging for clams until my fingers were raw. I remember our cousins ragging us about our Southern accents, mimicking our Texas twang and coaxing us to say, "Park your car in Harvard Yard." As soon as Uncle Warren walked in carrying sacks of hot, crispy clam cakes and cartons of "chowda" from Rocky Point, he put a stop to it. He only had to raise his voice once.

Warren had been a pilot and a POW during World War II, shot down over Austria during a bombing mission, liberated by General George G. Patton himself. Mother told us countless stories about the war, about the time a letter she'd sent a beau came back marked "Deceased." She didn't know what that meant, and Gram had to explain it to her. She said Warren never talked about the war, that the subject was taboo. "Warren called me 'Beautiful': 'Hello, Beautiful!' 'Want some fresh strawberries, Beautiful? It made me feel very special and boosted my morale no end."

I loved everything about the house, from the flowery wallpaper to the doilies on the furniture to the circular rag rugs Gram had braided from old discards. There was a glossy black piano in the sunroom, everything tied together by a huge brick fireplace where we once played contentedly with the bellows. I felt like a princess sleeping in Mom's old bedroom upstairs, lying in bed thinking back to stories from her childhood. Gram bought the Glen Avenue house with an inheritance after her father died.

Before that, times had been bleak. After Gram and my grandfather divorced, she worked in a shoe polish factory, a single mom living in a tenement with three children. Mother said she had to wear boy's clothes to school, and when she got sent home with head lice, Gram sheared off all her pretty curls until she looked like a boy. Mom was a lefty, but her teachers, all old maids, were so strict they made her use her right hand in class, swatting her hand with a ruler if she didn't obey. Then there was the "mud pie incident." Mom and a little friend from the tenement were making mud pies out in the yard. Mom talked her friend into eating one, and when the little girl died a week later, Mom felt responsible, confessing to Gram tearfully after the funeral. Gram reassured her that the family was very poor and that the girl's death wasn't her fault. Despite her diagnosis of adult-onset diabetes, Gram indulged our every whim, letting us pick out sweet treats from the bakery truck each morning, and introducing us to a whole new cuisine as she made blueberry pancakes or Johnny cakes, along with brown bread steamed in a coffee can, for breakfast, her voice tender as a lullaby. "Does that taste good to you, dahlin'?" she'd coo from across the table.

A full-figured woman, she stood five feet in her stocking feet. I never knew her to be without her stockings, her gray garters peeking out from the hem of her dress whenever she sat down. She was a real talker, never at a loss for words. And when she took the time to sit down to visit, she'd light up a cigarette, lost in conversation and oblivious to the gray cylinder of ash about to hit the floor until my mother whispered, "Your ash, Mom. Your ash."

When we didn't have company, Dad kept busy repairing Gram's storm windows or fixing leaky faucets. Since we happened to be in Rhode Island on his birthday, he was subjected to a nose-buttering, a Follett tradition that has long since died out. Dad was a good sport about it, and braced for it. He knew it was going to happen, just didn't know when it would happen. We managed to keep a straight face as Gram snuck up behind him at the breakfast table, a large yellow glob of butter at the ready in her cupped fingers. After slathering his nose to help him slide through another year, she howled with delight. It may have been the most fun I'd had during our visit: There's nothing better than a nose-buttering to break the tension of Mom's illness and her recovery.

Because of Mom's delicate condition, we weren't going to visit Uncle Ben and Aunt Elsie at their summer camp on Lake Champlain. There would be no sailing with my cousins, no sun-bathing on the dock, no ice-cold dunks at the shoreline, no skiing and no lobster dinners. This pleased Gram no end. She wasn't overly fond of her son's mother-in-law, muttering "Mrs. Simonds and her diamonds" every time the topic came up. After two weeks of reconnecting with the Follett clan—after the boiled dinners and baked swordfish and littleneck clams—we set out for Texas somewhat apprehensive about Mom's frame of mind. Mother had always been a woman-child, fragile as a spring flower. She couldn't watch the Alfred Hitchcock Hour unless I sat beside her on the sofa and held her hand, our roles irrevocably reversed. She had many phobias, including, but not limited to, crowds, elevators, and heights. Daddy took it all in stride, and we consoled her as best we could while she hyperventilated as we crossed the Brooklyn Bridge. She was withdrawn throughout the trip home, preoccupied with her own thoughts, unhappy with each motel we stopped at, counting her Milltowns each evening like an addict. Would she cut off our tails with a carving knife before we got home?

Uncle Warren's wife, my aunt Phyllis, once confided that all my mother ever wanted was to meet the man of her dreams and have a little girl named Susan. Although she got both, Texas seemed to be both the elixir and the sledgehammer of her life. Agoraphobic would have been a better word to describe my mother, for in the years that followed her hospitalization, she rarely ventured outside the house, phoning Dad at his office and reading off the grocery list. This didn't seem unusual to me, and life hummed along at a somewhat normal pace as I returned to school with a spring in my step, no worse for the experience. I had my mother back, compulsive hand washing and all.

My parents never lost their sense of humor, their occasional arguments turning light-hearted as they imitated Jackie Gleason on "The Honeymooners" with a drawn out "Shayutupppp" or a "One of these days...Pow, right in the kisser!" And when Mom wasn't visiting her shrink or getting her prescriptions filled, I might find her standing at her easel in the sunroom, a budding artist painting not what she *saw*, but what she *was*, snowy winter scenes reminiscent of her life back East, a process that brought her peace of mind.

Whenever I have a memory lapse, so common in middle age, I think about Mom's struggle—a young mother trying desperately to remember. We'd relive some family happening at the dinner table and she'd draw a blank, which was very frustrating at a time when we didn't have the Internet at our fingertips to enlighten us about her clinical depression. Her doctors had said she'd regain her memory with time, but she never did get all of her long-term memory back, never owned up to those spankings she dished out when we were kids. Though Milltown and Dexedrine had been Mom's coping tools early on post-treatment, she suffered a relapse after I got engaged. She had a difficult time accepting change of any kind, and by 1967, as my wedding day drew near, it became apparent she wouldn't attend. Those demons had her by the throat again, and she took to her bed the day of the service. Though I'd gone through a rebellious stage during my teen years, I was mature enough at that stage of life to let it go. Sure, it was awkward to say the least, but I never held this against her. There were some, however, who wouldn't or couldn't forgive her, including but not limited to my new mother-in-law and my new husband, later to become my ex-husband.

Following my divorce, after a decade living the life of a single mom, I got engaged to Mr. Right. And thanks to the more sophisticated meds on the market, all of Mom's demons had vaporized like dandelion spores in a summer wind. She happily attended my second wedding and had the time of her life. Though ever-changing antidepressants helped Mom cope with a thing she called her "nervous trouble," none of us were prepared for the emotional mayhem that ensued upon her death, a death that brought us to our collective knees. Mom was thirty-four years old when she wrote those letters from the hospital, seventy-two when she died. Congestive heart failure took her much too soon.

In the days, weeks, and months following Mom's funeral, we were in a quandary as to what to put on her headstone. It was Daddy who suggested *Loving Wife and Mother*. The day I saw her stone at City Cemetery in La Grange, somehow those four words didn't seem like enough. But years later, I discovered her letters while packing up my childhood home for Dad's move to a house across town. They were bundled together with faded yellow ribbon and tucked inside one of her dresser drawers. At the time, I felt certain that my father would find it much too painful to revisit that part of his life, so I tucked them away for safekeeping. When I finally felt strong enough to read them, I realized her epitaph made perfect sense.

Daddy, Uncle Ben, Mom, And My Brother

Chapter 8 – This Gun Is Loaded

*She was not accustomed to taste the joys of
solitude except in company.*

— EDITH WHARTON

During the Great Depression, it was commonplace for hobos riding the rails to jump off at our Fayette County ranch looking for handouts or a day's worth of work. My grandmother obliged them with mayonnaise sandwiches she passed through the back door of the house before sending them on their way. I still marvel at her wherewithal. Since I'm just an urban cowgirl, I'm not sure I could handle strangers wandering in to the isolated setting of the ranch.

Before East State Highway 71 came through, and there was no true road linking area townships, the gravel road on the outskirts of La Grange was about as far away as a football field from the ranch house. Whenever my grandmother was alone after dark, she grew uneasy with the thought that men driving to the notorious brothel known as the Chicken Ranch on the other side of Texas 71 might make a wrong turn and end up at the Blue Branch instead. My father told me this story some years after her death, adding that all the locals were on friendly terms with the madam,

Jessie Williams. During her reign in the 1930s, if folks happened to run into her in town, they'd wave and call out with a "Hi, Aunt Jessie. Hope you're doing well." Aunt Jessie was well liked in the community. And, being civic-minded, gave generously to help with the expansion of the local hospital and the creation of a public swimming pool in town.

During my youth, I never suspected the popular brothel was right under our noses, sitting on a parcel of land my grandparents once owned. It was never talked about. Not in my immediate family or by locals. I first heard about it while attending classes at Sam Houston State. How it was a rite of passage for young men. How during the Depression years, when money was tight, men could barter a laying hen for services—thus, the moniker. Even as a young woman, the subject was taboo until one misstep around the Sunday dinner table at my grandparents' Houston house. Granddad, always delighted to tell tales about his days on the Blue Branch, started carrying on about bartering firewood to the ladies at the Chicken Ranch back when they still cooked on a wood stove. Aunt Laura perked up, grinning from her end of the table when she asked him what he'd gotten in return. My grandmother, who'd picked up on the conversation from her vantage point in the kitchen, came into the dining room, grabbing Granddad by the elbow and escorting him from the room; the subject verboten, Granddad never mentioned the Chicken Ranch again.

In the summer of 1973, Marvin Zindler, an investigative reporter for KTRK in Houston, was the apocalypse that brought the Chicken Ranch down. A flashy dresser with a flamboyant personality who loved being in the spotlight, Zindler had been alerted by the Department of Public Safety that they had evidence the brothel was operating an organized crime ring. Although this information was totally unfounded—there wasn't even any alcohol on the premises, only a Coke machine—Zindler ran with the story, tangling with Jim Flournoy, the sheriff of Fayette County, on more than one occasion. Just months before Jessie Williams died in 1962, she sold out to a young prostitute by the name of Edna Milton. From what I understand, both had helped keep crime in the area under wraps using a private phone line to Sheriff Jim. Loose lips sink ships, and she'd inform the sheriff of any conversations the girls overheard that might lead to an arrest.

Sheriff Jim, a former Texas Ranger, was a tough old coot and tough on crime. I might add that he did *not* go riding off into the sunset with Edna Milton as did Burt Reynolds with Dolly Parton in the movie *The Best Little Whorehouse in Texas*. Far from it. A glitzy, glorified parody, the movie held many half-truths, the scenes shot in front of the actual Fayette County Courthouse the only thing *real* about it.

In 1974, a granite monument was dedicated to Sheriff Jim at the County Fairgrounds for his dedicated service. The inscription reads *Friend and Protector*. An 8 x10 glossy poster of Sheriff Jim posing on the monument—Burt Reynolds looked nothing like him, by the way—once hung on a wall of my father's office and now hangs in mine. Dressed in a gray suit and tie, a white Stetson and black cowboy boots, one arm resting on the stone, he's gazing stoically into the distance through his horn-rimmed glasses. These posters were printed in bulk and sold to raise money for Sheriff Jim's legal defense. Apparently, during one of their confrontations, he'd attacked Marvin Zindler, breaking a few ribs in the process. By 1976, under intense pressure from the governor, the Chicken Ranch was shuttered for good. But by 1980, after serving the county faithfully for more than thirty years, Sheriff Jim and his wife were so sick of the Chicken Ranch brouhaha that he resigned his post.

After a couple of Houston lawyers bought the ranch's main house and had it moved to Dallas, it made one last gasp as a restaurant, closing within a year. In the years that followed, I'd hike across Texas 71 with my cousins Pam and Lauran, and friends Kay and Fritzeen, posing for pictures in front of the ruins of the Chicken Ranch, where a few tattered rooms sat in weeds and decay, a weather-beaten backdrop to a patch of bluebonnets struggling to survive in the buckshot soil. Sometime later on, my uncle Ben, known for his pranks and mischief in general, made a strange request. Could my brother Ben collect some of the cedar shingles from the roof of what remained of the brothel in La Grange? To his delight, my brother obliged him with a box full. A note of thanks soon followed. Uncle Ben had used the shingles as trophies, handing them out at a tennis tournament held each summer at Starr Farm on Lake Champlain, Vermont, the participants tickled pink to get them.

Whenever I get back to Texas, once I leave the airport and the confines of the city, I feel like I'm back on the frontier. It always surprises me a little that the landscape filling my windshield reminds me of a Western movie set, everything wild and untamed. I can't help but think about the honky-tonk in the little town of Cut and Shoot where the bouncer at the front door checks you for guns as you enter. And if you don't already have a gun, they'll give you one. I don't know this for a *fact*, I just know that it's true. Guns have always been an integral part of the Texas landscape. And for good reason. Reasons that go far beyond early skirmishes with the Comanche and the Apache. When my geologist husband was working on oil rigs as a mud logger, his travels took him to remote areas across the state. While in training for Baroid, an oilfield service company, he learned about the dangers and the safety measures put in place should any lethal pockets of H2S gas (hydrogen sulfide) permeated the surface during the drilling process. More disturbing than the H2S gas so common in the eastern part of the state were other perils further west. An employee on his way to one of the rigs had been jumped and killed, his throat slashed after he left his car to open a gate.

After a co-worker cautioned Dan to carry a pistol for protection, he took it seriously. He was working a night shift on a rig thirty miles outside of Freer, a small South Texas town an hour's drive from Laredo. Each evening he'd drive the last eleven miles of his commute on a deserted caliche road leading to the rig, opening and closing gates as he went, a flashlight in one hand and a .357 Smith & Wesson in the other. Damned if he'd be the victim of a *deguello*, Spanish for throat-cutting. Giant rattlesnakes, mangy coyotes, the occasional badger and herds of javelina were a common sight. And so many jackrabbits he quit hitting his brakes to miss them. One night, right after he'd secured a gate and stepped back into his car, a murky form appeared in his headlights some twenty feet away. He breathed a sigh of relief as a mountain lion crossed the path and wandered off into the darkness. No *deguello* that night.

Ben did a lot of field work for Dad after he retired from Amoco and started his own company, Global Surveyors. I never knew my brother to carry a gun unless he was hunting. But I imagine he'd wished for one during one of his surveys outside of Navasota, a quiet little town about seventy miles northwest of Houston. The property owner requesting the survey was putting together a private zoo, not an uncommon venture in

Texas. And with llamas roaming the grounds, Ben was at the tail end of the chain, taking measurements as he passed by a large oblong cage that, unbeknownst to him, held a Bengal tiger at the far end. The members of the survey crew up ahead must have awakened the tiger in passing, never bothering to radio Ben about it. By the time he got even with the cage, the tiger charged full steam ahead, hitting the flimsy wire with a big roar. The chicken-wire bent six feet outward but thankfully held. A heart-stopping moment for Ben, to put it mildly. Later on, the property owner apologized profusely, explaining that he'd been working on a better cage and would finish it very soon.

In August of 1999, I got my first taste of uneasiness at our ranch. In June of that year, the Railway Killer had brutally murdered the Sirnics, a couple who lived in Weimar, only minutes by rail from the Blue Branch. The train tracks are close to the house and the cabin, and I cautioned my father to keep the doors locked even if he just stepped out to tend his garden. While the killing spree continued, the face of Angel Resendiz flashed across the six o'clock news and appeared on the *America's Most Wanted* TV program. As Resendiz blew across the state like the breath of Satan, the paranoia in Fayette County became palpable. In one of our phone conversations Dad said the local gun shop was running out of guns and ammunition. I hardly slept a wink until a Texas Ranger captured Resendiz at the Mexican border and put him behind bars. It was estimated that Resendiz had taken the lives of fifteen people. He was indicted for the rape and murder of Claudia Benton, a young doctor who'd lived a few blocks from our Houston home.

In the spring of 2002, we learned that crime doesn't always have a name or a face after the sheriff in La Grange received a distress call from a woman who said that her estranged husband was on his way from Waco to kill her. One high-speed chase on the outskirts of town later, the sheriff lost the suspect after his truck flipped and rolled down an embankment near the entrance to our ranch.

The bandit disappeared into the night on foot, kicking in the same back door my grandmother had fed so many hobos through. While deputies searched the grounds of the Blue Branch in the wee hours, he was watching their every move from inside. Apparently they couldn't search the house without a warrant, and it was a stroke of luck that my brother and father were away on business at the time.

It wasn't the kind of thing the media picked up on. There'd been no press coverage on the local nightly news, but after the robber cashed some of Dad's checks, the Texas Rangers got in on the action. I thought for sure they'd nail him, but during my visit a month later he was still on the loose. Up until then it had been an exciting tale to tell friends, but shortly after I stepped from the car during my visit, reality set in. My brother had replaced the pretty glass door that was original to the house with an ugly-but-safe solid wood door with a double dead-bolt lock. I hated the new door and what it represented. Might as well hang up a sign that says Paranoia Rules! Ben and Dad gave me more details about the break-in right up until bedtime. Very little had been disturbed inside the house—no food eaten—so the authorities had nicknamed him the "Neat Thief." Despite the moniker, he'd stolen every box of .22 bullets he could find, so we knew he was armed and dangerous. Even more disturbing was the fact that, according to an investigator on the case, the Neat Thief had made numerous phone calls describing the ranch to some of his friends. After Dad and I retired to the cabin and I prepared for bed, I resented this scoundrel for destroying my peace of mind.

Dad always stressed gun safety to us in our early years, and I thought about that as I eyed the gun rack above my bed where a yellow sticky note on the stock of the deer rifle read: *Warning. This gun is loaded.* Written in Dad's precise hand, the note was a chilling reminder of those infamous days of the Railway Killer, left there for *us*, not a would-be robber. I woke up the next morning sleep deprived as we discussed the possibility of an alarm system.

"We never locked the doors in all the years I lived here," Dad said, somewhat dazed. "In fact, if a family member or a friend dropped by and found us gone, they'd leave something amiss, like turning a chair upside down or placing it on top of a table. Then, if we ran into them in town, they'd ask if we'd found it and we'd all laugh about it."

"I guess those days are long gone," I said.

Dad's coffee is strong enough to float lug nuts, but that day I needed the jolt. The weather report promised some much-needed rain, but we watered the vegetable garden anyway before Dad decided to drive into town to buy a new rain gauge.

"It hasn't rained in so long I forgot where I put the other one," he smiled before driving off.

I met my brother inside the house right before he dashed outside, asking me in passing whether I needed anything from the HEB. And just like that, for the first time in my memory, I was alone at the ranch. If not for the mitigating circumstances it might not have bothered me, but there I was in broad daylight alone with no car and feeling vulnerable as a newborn.

I locked the new door and paced from room to room. In my favor were guns at my disposal, and I reached up to touch the deer rifle in the rack on my nephew's bedroom wall. Was the safety on or off? I clicked it once or twice. Was it loaded? No sticky note attached to the stock of this one. My brother, son, and nephews are all excellent marksmen, but I have to admit that I'm no Annie Oakley. I know my way around guns somewhat. I've tagged along on dove hunts, shot a few snakes and join in on some target practice occasionally. But I've never had the patience or the heart to sit in a deer blind waiting for some unsuspecting buck to come eat corn from the feed store. If confronted by an intruder, finding myself in a panic-ridden state of self-defense, could I pull the trigger? Worse yet, would I be *tested*? The deer rifle only gave me a false sense of security.

Crime is something that happens to other people, until, of course, it happens to you. I tried reasoning with myself that nothing was going to happen, all the while thinking about the Neat Thief. I didn't have a clue what he looked like. What if he or one of his gunslinger friends comes back? Imagining myself in a fit of bravery, I thought about one of the opening lines from an episode of *Have Gun – Will Travel*. Richard Boone pulls out his revolver, points it toward the camera and says, "I'd like you to take a look at this gun. The balance is excellent. This trigger responds to the pressure of one ounce. The gun was handcrafted to my specifications, and I rarely draw it unless I mean to use it."

I was busy contemplating whether my survival instincts would be put to the test when Dad drove up and my brother soon followed. My little drama had ended, and we fell into our normal routine of mowing, treating pond scum and poisoning fire ant mounds. For periods of time things felt normal again until I walked to the house expecting to see my grandmother's pretty glass door, the one that still locked with the old skeleton key. If my grandmother were alive she'd say that it could have been worse. But the new door is a constant reminder of what could have been.

The next day I borrowed Dad's Suburban to run some errands of my own. "There's a pistol under the driver's seat," he said, handing me the keys. "And it's loaded." I nodded on my way out, picturing my grandmother parked at the cattle guard in the middle of the night with the motor running, the high beams pointed toward the highway, her habit when Granddad worked the late shift.

Whether she was armed I couldn't say, but I left the ranch wondering if our lives there will ever be quite the same again. 🌿

Sheriff Jim Flournoy, 1975. Courtesy of Fayette County Fair Association

Chapter 9 – Aunt Edna And The Road
Less Traveled

…the world's so finely
Balanced a beetle could push it along

— FIDDLEDEEDEE, BY SHELBY STEPHENSON

A Sunday drive can sometimes take you places you'd least expect. So, on a blistering Sunday in August of 2003, to make up for another dull afternoon sitting next to the window unit in the cabin, I set out with Dad on a mindless ramble across Fayette County, the pump jack in the front pasture lending a certain ugliness to the ranch, the riparian grasses still trying to make a comeback since the drilling; the pasture, once vibrant with wildflowers and buffalo grass, was now barren as the moon.

There's a no-burn ban due to the drought, clumps of prickly pear cactus and a scattering of live oaks and cedars the only relief of green against an otherwise dead landscape. I don't know what the temperature is outside, but with the sun beating through the windows it feels like we're driving across the Sahara Desert even with the AC running full blast.

"We couldn't buy a breath of fresh air today if our lives depended on it," Dad says.

On a lark, we decide to drive to the county fairgrounds, where an attempt is under way to preserve some of the Czech history in the form of a Cultural Center. Dad chuckles that the name Cultural Center seems like a misnomer, that he never knew any Czechs who had any money. The Texas Hill Country was settled by Germans and Czechs, and though it isn't the norm now, in my youth the German language thrived from the fairgrounds to the courthouse square.

As we wheel past the deserted dance hall, I can almost hear the walls thumping out a polka. Every Labor Day weekend, the fairgrounds come alive as the Fayette County Fair gets underway. It was always an exciting time for me and my brother as we walked the livestock exhibits, ate cotton candy, and bought tickets for the Ferris wheel or the merry-go-round, the midway crawling with barkers and young people throwing softballs at milk jugs or darts at a wall of balloons. The fair has been going on since the beginning of time. One treasure passed down to me is a glass chick of royal blue that my grandfather won at a penny pitch when he was a boy. For as long as I can remember, my grandparents stored kitchen matches in the small well behind the chick's head.

Ordinarily, I avoid Texas in the summer, but Dad just celebrated his eighty-fifth birthday and the heat is the least of my worries. Behind the wheel of his Suburban, he's fearless as any teenager. He wants to explore every trail that resembles a road, plunging down a rutted gravel path behind the exhibit halls. As we creep deeper and deeper into the woods, with saw briers and grape vines scraping against the doors, the road narrows, then dead-ends with no turnaround. I clutch the doorknob preparing for a hasty exit while he backs the Suburban out over a steep drop-off. With a paralyzing view of the Colorado River far below us, the rear wheels spinning and rocks flying, we might put a new twist on Robert Frost's poem, "The Road Not Taken."

After we gain purchase and retreat, we decide we'll drive over to Aunt Edna's ranch. Edna Hoefer is Dad's aunt through marriage, the sister of his aunt Millie Hoefer, who married his uncle Elo Schaefer, brother to my grandmother Perry. Because there's an unwritten law in Fayette

County that says one never drops in on friend or family empty-handed, we pull into Lukas Bakery for a small bag of sugar cookies.

One more a pit-stop at the Quickie Mart for a Miller Lite and an Eskimo Pie and we're on our way again, weaving to the north end of town while he phones Edna and pours beer into a Styrofoam cup. There's no answer but we keep driving anyway, speeding around the Austin bypass toward Monument Hill State Park and Edna's place, my ice cream dripping into a soggy napkin.

We pass the golf course and a 1950's-era subdivision of native limestone and brick houses overlooking the river. So many new ranch houses have appeared along the highway since my last visit that I hardly recognize the area. Our turf has been diluted with weekenders from Houston, their faux ranches pictures of architectural splendor, hard to miss with their impressive iron entry gates and whimsical scenes of cacti, windmills, and coyotes, along with equally whimsical names. We turn onto a secondary road before turning again onto the gravel road leading to Edna's ranch, stopping once to look at the hard-scrabble land that my paternal great-grandparents once farmed. It's the only landmark I recognize, and the weekend retreat that's appeared since our last trip looks out of place on the piece of property Granny Perry once called Poor Joe's. I'd be hard-pressed to find Edna's place on my own, and the twisting gravel road seems to go on and on. I wonder aloud if this is where the term "distant relative" came from when a spit of rain on the windshield opens up a path in Dad's mind as well.

"Before the roads were paved, everybody packed up and left at the first sign of a sprinkle. One day when we returned to the farm after a shower, I started to cry because we didn't get stuck in the mud. My folks laughed about it, but that was a big adventure to a kid back then. In today's world kids would turn to their smart phones until Triple A arrived," he says with a chuckle.

Edna's house sits high atop a steep hill. When Dad was a kid, he took a rollercoaster ride from the top after popping the emergency brake on in his folks' Model A. At one time it was a working cattle ranch but it never had a formal name. Folks called it the Schaefer Place and a century later it's become the Old Schaefer Place. The house hasn't changed any since my youth, although Dad said that it once had a second floor that got knocked off in a storm. Apparently money was tight, so rather than rebuild, my maternal great-grandparents roofed over the first floor. The paint has long since assumed the gray patina of barn wood, and rusty tin cans overflowing with aloes and ghost plants hang under the eaves where they'll catch rainwater.

The house reminds me of the old saying, "Too poor to paint, too proud to whitewash." It looks like one strong gust of wind might flatten it. As we cross the low-water bridge over a dry creek, my great-uncle Elo comes alive again in my memory. A stocky man partial to bib overalls, he'd walk down the hill to greet us, his accent thick from the Fatherland. (The *Neu-Braunsfelser Zeitung*, a German newspaper, was in circulation until 1954, about the time of that visit.)

No visit was complete without a trip to Elo's smokehouse where he'd proudly show off his venison sausage, handing a few links to Dad. Elo was the youngest boy to four older sisters, including my grandmother, and I'd heard he was a wild child in his youth, rolling smokes at the age of nine, skipping school at every opportunity and thumbing his nose at anything that even remotely *resembled* work. Though he managed to woo and marry Emillie Hoefer, a hardworking German girl, he never left home, and took to making bootleg whiskey during the Prohibition years. Known for his barroom brawls, he did some jail time, but stayed one step ahead of the law at all times, and nobody in the family has ever figured out where he hid his still.

The house looks deserted, with two cars of ancient vintage up to their axles in weeds, left in the yard ages ago to discourage intruders. The 1960 Impala parked under a shed says that Edna is around *somewhere*. I'm a little tense about showing up unannounced until Edna appears, all smiles, clutching my shoulders with a vice grip and drawing me to her ample bosom. She never married, and I know she misses the companionship of her sister Millie, who passed away some years back.

I couldn't take the isolation of rural life, but it seems to agree with Edna as she rattles off the events that make up a typical day: Her tractor's on the blink. It may have a cracked head. One of her bulls has gone lame. She hopes to nurse him back to health so she can sell him. There's a problem with her windmill. The cistern is leaning and she can't find anybody to come fix it—all this from a woman two month's shy of her ninetieth birthday.

There's a wringer washing machine on the porch, and like the outside of the house, little has changed inside. The green linoleum has been worn down to the floorboards, leaving dark trails that run from room to room. The old staircase just off the parlor dead-ends at the ceiling like something out of *Lemony Snicket's: A Series of Unfortunate Events* books. Unless you consider a portable TV with rabbit ears, a telephone and a ceiling fan luxury items, there are few to be found here. The same iron bed my great-grandparents slept in is visible from our cramped sitting area, two pot-bellied stoves fueled exclusively by wood from the property the only source of heat. Self-sufficiency is more than a doctrine here, it's a proverb.

Dressed in brown polyester slacks and a white shirt, Edna runs a hand through her close-cropped hair, apologizing for the state of the house before she and Dad start reliving the days they spent chopping cotton and topping corn during their youth. Normally there's a stiff breeze up on the hill but I'm breaking out in a sweat. In this no-frills atmosphere, I notice that a fly swatter hanging nearby has been patched. Spry for her age, Edna's tanned face is remarkably free from the hard lines you'd associate with ranch life. She seems content with her lot, and I savor the moment knowing that hers is the last German accent I will ever hear, at least from a member of my family. At one time the kitchen shelves sagged under the weight of preserves she and Aunt Millie put up. She'd always hand me a jar of her dill pickles as a parting gift. I got their recipe years before, along with fresh dill from their garden, but try as I might, mine turned out like those kerosene cucumbers Aunt Bee entered at the Mayberry County Fair.

When Edna and Millie ran their café in La Grange, the ingredients for most everything they served, from the fried chicken to the chili, came from their ranch. But Edna says she shops at the HEB now that she's alone. She tells us that Dad's cousin Gladys passed away last year and one thing leads to another:

"Remember ven her son Jeffrey died playing football? He vas hit in der chest with der ball. Such a tragedy! His mudder and fadder worshipped him."

This is the *third* version of the story I've heard. I thought he died of heat stroke during football practice. We didn't make it to Floresville very often, so I hadn't seen Jeff since he was a little kid. But I do remember the shockwaves his death sent throughout our family. I was away at school at the time, and Dad said that Aunt Tillie was so distraught over her grandson that she collapsed and broke her hip leaving the funeral home. The last time I'd seen Gladys, she was drowning her sorrows in a bottle of Maker's Mark at the Cottonwood Inn. But that was a long time ago.

A clap of thunder in the distance seems to be our signal to depart, and we go through the motions of leaving for some time, lingering in the side yard with the promise of rain while a pump jack on the next ranch dips to the ground like the head of a giant fossilized bird. Another clap of thunder as we cross back over the low-water bridge brings Elo's death to the forefront of my memory. I was just a young girl the night my grandmother called with the news in the fall of 1957. And it wasn't so much his death as the *way* he died that shook me to the core. As I remember it, Elo had gone into town to pick up Millie and Edna at the café at closing time, as he did most evenings. They drove to the ranch in a downpour, and when they reached the bridge, the normally dry creek was boiling. In the glow of the headlights, Elo walked out on the bridge to check it, and when he did, the bridge collapsed beneath him, pinning his foot. Despite their heroic efforts, Millie and Edna couldn't save Elo from the rushing water, the current nearly overpowering them. Dad said it's a wonder they didn't all drown that night, and the image still haunts me.

On the drive home, Dad makes a comment about the clutter on the front porch and how people who don't have visitors tend to let things go. No doubt there are those who'd find the state of Edna's house off-putting. Granted, it's a fire trap with no smoke detectors. But during our visit I was silently dusting off the cobwebs of my own life and taking stock. I *like* knowing there's a place within driving distance where, say, "megabyte" isn't a word, a place that's managed to escape the drumbeat of time. Like Elo, Edna is living her best life, and the day will come when their kind will be lost to the ages. ❧

Postscript: The last time I visited Aunt Edna was in the fall of 2008. Recuperating from a broken hip, she managed to walk the grounds with a cane, glad to be out of rehab and back home again. In the summer of 2013, Edna and her younger sister appeared in an article in *Texas Monthly* about the passing of a dialect. That fall, she celebrated her 100th birthday at a nursing home in La Grange. My brother said that Edna's mind that day was still pretty sharp, though she didn't recognize my two nephews and probably wouldn't have recognized me any longer. He said when the party ended, she begged him not to leave. Edna died in May of 2016 at the age of 102. The old ranch house is deserted now, an iron gate securely locked to keep out any trespassers.

At this writing, the parcel of land known as the Schaefer Place is destined to be sold, the money divided between the heirs, "the road less traveled" destined to become just another memory.

Auf Wiedershen, Aunt Edna.

Back row, left to right: Kerry, Aunt Millie, Aunt Edna.
Front row, left to to right: Kerry's friend Lance and Benjie, 1970s.

Chapter 10 – Grouse Moor

...this is life, and there is no theory for it...

— FIDDLEDEEDEE, BY SHELBY STEPHENSON

There comes a time in most of our adult lives when a parent is diagnosed with some debilitating illness, or their health fails in some way, and you have to make the dreaded decision to put one or both in a rest home, or an assisted living facility as they're called today. I've never had to face that. My father is healthy and alert, and at the age of eighty-four, still puts in a forty-hour work week. My dilemma started in the spring of 2004 with the Grouse Moor house.

My son, Kerry, saw the house before I did. It was the one my father gave me such glowing reports about, the one he bought in East Jesus at the wrong end of nowhere after selling my childhood home in Houston, a home centrally located and convenient to everything including the Texas Medical Center. I listened patiently while Kerry suffered a meltdown over the phone. His lament started with the age of the house (at least thirty years old), and the fact that it was in dire need of repairs; his estimate to get it up to snuff was about five grand. I knew

85

he'd been having trouble adjusting to the idea of his Gramper living in a new place, in a new neighborhood, like we all had, and hung up dreading my next visit. I'd had misgivings about the location early on, as Highway 6 is a long commute through heavy traffic to Dad's office. Cathy, my ex sister-in-law, handled the sale, so I had some inside information as to why he'd sold the family home and chosen the Grouse Moor house, and it boiled down to his new girlfriend and paying off some of his debt. Bear Creek has its upscale areas, but the house on Grouse Moor Street was just another cookie-cutter house in an aging blue collar neighborhood. Dad had been holding back key information, but if I crawled under his skin for a second, I could see the draw. He'd said time and again, "It's no fun seeing the Grand Canyon alone." It was a fresh start for him, and an escape from loneliness. I learned that Cathy had shown them much nicer homes, but Dad's girlfriend insisted on this one.

My first walk-though filled me with rage. The great room looked like a band of derelicts on a psilocybin high decided to replicate the great outdoors, painting the walls a hideous shade of blue before airbrushing white clouds at random from ceiling to floor. Maybe in the Sistine Chapel, but, seriously? All I could think about was rolling some Martha Stewart Living paint in a muted shade of Cotswold Green or Village Tan over the whole affair. Sliding glass doors across the back of the room opened onto a sunken yard that probably flooded with every Houston rain. Except for a solitary oak tree at the fence, the yard had no plantings to give it character, and it took all my strength to pry the sliding door open just enough to squeeze through. I kept thinking *Fire Hazard*, *Fire Trap*, and from the looks of the charred cabinet next to the stove, a grease fire of epic proportions had taken place before those hippies left.

All the things Kerry had told me clicked, from the rusty gnarled racks in the dishwasher, to the mysterious dripping noise inside the bathroom wall, to the outdated AC unit moaning in its struggle to keep up with the Houston heat, to the sliding glass door in the master bedroom that was frozen shut. While Kerry got busy burying plastic drainage pipes around the perimeter of the patio to keep the great room from flooding during a downpour, I wondered how the house had ever passed inspection in the first place. I didn't know whether to laugh hysterically or strangle Cathy for showing Daddy the house to begin with.

The rooms were empty for the most part, and I gathered at some point the young girlfriend would be filling them up with her own stuff, including her two kids. After my mom died, I knew Dad would be vulnerable. Widowhood is rough on men, and my father is a very social person. After some time passed and he confided that he'd been dating an old girlfriend from high school, I encouraged it. Dad had always been the quintessential Ward Cleaver: an articulate and dedicated office worker, devoted family man of wit and fairness, full of patience and understanding. When I thought of his current girlfriend and the situation he was in, I had to dig deep to find some of that understanding within myself.

Though I knew all his defenses were down, I never pegged him a Casanova who'd take up with a woman young enough to be my daughter. We've always had a great propensity in our family for giving each other sound advice, then not heeding any of it. From the outside looking in, everyone knew the odds. She was an uneducated divorcee with no job or any career plans in desperate need of financial help, a gold-digger my father just happened to meet as he passed her desk one day at a secretarial service he used from time to time.

Typically, whenever I complained of the age difference to my male friends, they'd give a high-five sign as if to say "More power to him." It didn't tarnish my image of him as much as it brought into focus his loneliness and vulnerability, and I felt tremendous guilt for living so far away. Though I tried to look on the bright side, the future for him didn't look so bright. Whenever a friend or distant relative asked about him, I lied about the situation completely. It was just too embarrassing. The house held only the dregs from our Riley Street house, and the sleeper sofa and easy chair Cathy and her husband had delivered earlier looked lost in the empty great room. Between the barking Rottweiler next door, the mysterious dripping noises, and the groaning heat pump, sleep was impossible.

Lying there in the darkness, I thought about the day I got a distraught phone call from Dad. His girlfriend had had an accident involving a "dinner ring" he'd given her. Apparently, she'd been jumping from the floor to flip an AC vent at the ceiling, and the ring got caught between the slats, ripping off the first joint of her ring finger on her trip down. Bad karma? Maybe. I couldn't help wondering if the ring had been my mother's diamond solitaire, the one Kerry found during the Big Move. And I never understood why her finger wasn't reattached when surgeons in Houston were reattaching whole arms and legs that had been caught in thrashing machines. Red flags began flapping wildly.

Our Christmas visit was another truckload of emotional chowchow. My father's new love had moved in with her ready-made family and a fake tree from Walmart. Her small son had the haunted look of a lost puppy, and when I learned that the cases of Ramen noodles stacked in the kitchen were the only things he'd eat, I understood why. The teenaged daughter holed up in her room, ignoring us completely. There wasn't a picture of us anywhere about the house, only *her* pictures. We'd been erased from the equation that was our old life together, our typical nuclear family disintegrated with one blow. The red poinsettia I'd brought clashed with the pink Christmas decorations, but trying to make the best of a strained situation, I opened the tin of Russian tea cakes I'd baked. When she pulled a cookie sheet of green Pillsbury sugar cookies from the oven, I knew we could never be friends.

Refusing politely to stay over, Kerry and I bounced back and forth like a couple of orphans between my sister-in-law's house and the cabin in La Grange. My brother refused to go to Grouse Moor at all. That we showed any outward signs of approval tore at my very soul. My only hope was that somehow this fling would run its course without depleting my father's bank account, and for a while it looked as though my deepest wish might come true. Months later, Dad talked like the situation with her had gotten out of hand, but he wouldn't say much beyond that.

The following June I was sitting at the dining table of my North Carolina home when I got a call from the Galvez Hotel in Galveston. Dad and his new bride were honeymooning there, and they wanted to pop the good news on me from afar. He sounded like he'd been drinking, heavily. What could I say? I stammered, wished them well, and got the lowdown in an email from my cousin Pam. They'd slipped off to the courthouse downtown under a veil of secrecy, with my cousin Gordon standing up for Dad, and a strung-out hooker wearing short-shorts stood up for her. It was almost more than I could bear.

My husband said the first time Dad stumbled, she'd be gone. But I dismissed it until months later when he fractured his hip riding a four-wheeler over a bumpy pasture. My dad's a very private person, so I had to read between the lines with every phone call. I'd assumed his bride would be taking care of him, but I assumed wrong. After Cathy told me about the split, I started checking last-minute flights. But after assessing the situation further, decided he'd be better off licking his wounds without me. His pride and embarrassment were much too raw. Cathy took him to the hospital for an outpatient procedure, and he recuperated at her house over Thanksgiving. I sent a flower arrangement, and when Dad was back on his feet, he revealed the reason for the split. He'd caught his bride smoking crack at the Grouse Moor house and given her an ultimatum that she later broke. "That explains the dingbat move with the AC vent," I remember thinking.

We were all holding our collective breath until the divorce was final, but Dad must have been born under a lucky star, for his bride didn't contest anything or try to take his property. Under great duress, he'd already signed the deed to the Blue Branch over to Ben and the grandsons. She did keep the Jeep Cherokee, however, and ran up a healthy amount of credit card debt. After I heard some of the horror stories about crack parties at the house during Dad's absence, I was ready to shout "crack whore" from the highest rooftops and call Adult Protective Services.

At our urging, he revised his will, protecting himself legally, and come spring, the house on Grouse Moor had gone through another metamorphosis. Liza had moved in with her two schnauzers, followed by Kenny, an old family friend. Liza, another single mom, had done some secretarial work for Dad, and Kenny, a washed-up drummer who never made it to the big time, was out of work in upstate New York. I learned from Cathy that he'd borrowed the money from Dad to make the move, and she felt like he'd turned into a hippie child living in a house with anyone who wanted to be there. To my surprise, Kenny found a job as a care-giver right away and started paying rent. He cooked and cleaned and despite the yapping dogs always underfoot, the house had taken on a new air with Liza's tasteful, overstuffed furniture.

We never saw much of Liza. She kept to herself. Apparently, her life away from the office consisted of trips to Blockbuster and weekends in front of the TV in her bedroom. Since Kenny worked the night shift, Dad rarely saw either of them except at mealtime. What seemed like a good setup in the beginning ended some five months later when they both moved out. Liza and Kenny didn't hit it off, and Kenny decided to move in with his newfound love across town.

When I met Kerry and his girlfriend there in August to celebrate Dad's eighty-third birthday, the house was a wreck, a catastrophe. Rafts of dog hair had collected under the furniture, and the deflated swimming pool they'd left out back had turned into a breeding ground for mosquitoes. The garage was full of the discards from two garage sales, along with the ex-wife's cast-off furniture. We all pitched in and spent the better part of two days cleaning, making household repairs, and hauling stuff to the dump. Kerry and Jennifer slept on camp mattresses in the lost puppy's vacant room, but Jennifer felt bad vibes the first night and dragged her sleeping pad out to the living room. I don't think either of us slept a wink, and the few times I dozed off I dreamed I'd sunk to the bottom of a deep well and couldn't claw my way to the top.

On our last night there, we hosted a small dinner party and invited Cathy and Steve over to see our handiwork. I set our old maple drop-leaf table with my mother's Blue Willow dinnerware and placed some of the cups and saucers on the empty shelving above the windows. On a side trip to the Blue Branch, we'd picked up some framed wall prints at a church rummage sale, and Cathy marveled at the changes. Though his physical therapy had ended, Dad was still using a cane, but we found an exercise machine like the one he'd been using in therapy and set it up in his bedroom. He seemed happy and relieved about the general outcome of everything.

I booked a flight to Houston the following Christmas, and Kerry said he'd meet me there on Christmas Eve. Everything was set, and I was elated about the upcoming holidays until Dad phoned one morning from his office. His ex-wife had fallen on hard times and moved back into the Grouse Moor house. The witch was back, and the shock of it blew through me like thunder. My father and I have always been close, but I felt more like a star-crossed lover than his daughter, so upset that I said I wouldn't be coming for Christmas at all and hung up.

Friends and family understood my feelings, but the hardest thing for me was telling my son. He'd threatened to strangle the ex if she ever did anything to hurt Gramper. I sent his girlfriend, Jennifer, an email and waited. Kerry took it about as hard as I thought he would, tearful when he got the news. After a week of stewing in my own juices, I decided to go ahead with my trip. If I didn't, it meant that she'd won. I phoned Dad at work to apologize and much to my relief, he chuckled.

He said that her move was only temporary until she could get back on her feet again, that she was selling hand-crafted jewelry at the local flea markets, and would be spending the holidays with her family. My son said he'd come as long as he didn't have to spend one waking second in the Grouse Moor house, and Jennifer was on the fence about the whole thing. I couldn't blame her.

The following spring, I was surprised with two new additions to the Grouse Moor house: a Siberian husky compliments of the ex, along with a gerbil resting quietly in an aquarium in the great room. I felt like I'd been caught up in one of those Monty Python skits when they march across the stage shouting, "And now for something completely different!" The house reeked of gerbil litter and Princess was riddled with fleas. Dad said he'd read that yeast was good for repelling fleas, but he'd been giving the husky Fleishmann's instead of the pet store variety. I've never been a dog person and found this jumper especially annoying. Though I felt like pulling my hair out, I hate watching any animal suffer. I made a mad dash to the drug store for flea shampoo, room foggers and air fresheners. Left alone all day, it was obvious Princess was starved for affection. I managed to break her bad jumping habit, and as time wore on, I could see she'd bonded with Dad and vice versa, so touching to see her curled up at his bedroom door at night, a faithful companion and a good watch dog.

From the lack of activity in the aquarium the last day of my stay, I realized the gerbil had gone to gerbil heaven. We gave it a proper burial in the curb-side garbage can, and I spent my waking hours picking through the fridge and tossing out moldy cheese, curdled milk, and a piece of cake that looked like a sponge from the Dead Sea. Dad managed to pick up a sofa and end tables at a yard sale, and except for the slanting waterbed I'm to sleep on, and the two or three empty hangers in the closet, my room is as barren as a prison cell. Even though I washed all the linens, I'll be the first to admit that I'm a tad OCD when it comes to sleeping on a used mattress with no apparent lineage. Every trip is a crusade to put the house back together, and I usually leave more stressed than when I arrived.

I feel that keeping up with a house and a yard, plus his full-time job and the commute, is just more than Dad can handle. Though he worries about making mistakes at the survey office, he's determined to stay active and says that mowing the grass is good exercise, that if he lets the yard go he gets nasty notes from the Homeowners Association. I try not to get in the way, and tell him that I just want him to be happy. Whether or not he'll find it *here* remains to be seen. At least it isn't a crack house any more.

With enough frequent flyer miles for a free trip, I phoned Dad about a spring visit. Whenever I call he complains that we have a bad connection, that he can't hear me, so it's apparent his hearing's shot. He said that Princess dug under the back yard fence recently and went missing. She was last spotted miles away in the HEB parking lot. And Liza has been making noises about moving back in with her two schnauzers. Already, more brush fires to put out. ✥

Mom in a moment of relaxation (Author photo)

Chapter 11 – The Cabin Revisited

And through it all you learn to live and laugh.
To make your own stories to pass on to those
Who look a little like you…

— TEXAS POETRY CALENDAR 2015 BY MARGARET DORNAUS

In August of 2004, I'm in the passenger seat of the Suburban with Dad at the wheel. He's just celebrated his eighty-fourth birthday and we're heading for the Blue Branch, an hour's drive from his new house in Bear Creek. A wet spring has brought an abundance of hay, and the harvested bales remind me of giant rolls of shredded wheat dumped haphazardly from a cereal box. I wish I could relax and enjoy the scenery, but Dad's erratic driving has me petrified. He had cataract surgery on his left eye in March, and he's never been a good driver to begin with. I'm convinced that boys who were raised on farms and ranches never make good drivers. It doesn't help that his cell phone keeps chirping: He forgot to put his seal on a survey. Another chirp: There's a boundary dispute on a lot in West University Place. He rings off, but can't seem to keep the Suburban between the lines, drifting over to the passing lane time and again, oblivious to the guy in the red pick-up flipping us the bird. "You need to move over," I caution, motioning toward the driving lane while he looks at me as if he's trying to read my lips. "Move over! And keep your eyes on the road!" His dog, Princess, is curled up in the back seat. Her ears, triangles of blond fur, are standing at attention. I've raised my voice again and I hate myself for it. The Suburban is his last bastion of independence, but the day is coming, and coming fast. Crossing the Colorado River Bridge, I envision us crashing through the guard rail and going air-born before plunging into the murky green water far below. Since he disconnected the alarm system, the Suburban's electric windows and door locks only work sporadically. In my mind's eye we're trapped inside, sinking ever so slowly to the bottom.

We stop for a bag of ice and groceries in the town of Ellinger. More of a bump in the road than a town, this is Dad's happy place because he knows the woman who bought the run-down gas station-grocery for a song and is now making hay faster than she can spend it. They chat at the counter while I pick up a box of *kolaches,* the German version of a Danish pastry, cheese being his favorite. Back in the car, I suggest that *maybe* I should take over the wheel.

Luckily for me, his new paramour isn't coming. Her excuses to stay behind remind me of that *Mayberry RFD* episode when Andy's blind date, Lydia, says: "I hate the outdoors. When I go outdoors, I get hives." Or, "I hate chit-chat. I like ordinary conversation, but I hate chit-chat." Even Dad has admitted quite reluctantly that she has "more flats than sharps", but he seems quite attached to her young son in a fatherly way.

A thermometer nailed to a hackberry tree at a corner of the cabin reads 100 degrees, the glassed-in porch hot enough to melt horse shoes. I flick on the window unit and toss the bag of ice into a cooler. A small chest freezer has taken the place of the old ice box, a piece of Styrofoam taped to the lid preventing the sun from working it to death. The plastic grocery bags draped over the corners are the feat of an engineer's mind: They keep the seals from leaking.

There's a red, cone-shaped gas fireplace in one corner and director's chairs lined up along a folding table that serves as Dad's makeshift drafting table, a task light illuminating the survey work that's been his life. Dad's collection of antique tools—a branding iron, rusty spurs, and horseshoes among them—are nailed across the front wall, the rest sitting chock-a-block on the dusty window ledges. Since mud daubers are so scarce, I'm hesitant to pry off the golf-ball-sized dauber nest glued to the lampshade. With mother gone, the cabin lacks a woman's touch. And I can't remember the last time these faded blue walls have seen a fresh coat of paint. Since the Blue Branch is home base now, and the heat's driving us indoors, I make a decision to paint. But when I grab the car keys for the trip to Farmers Lumber, Dad says he's lost his wallet. He can't find it anywhere. He's frantic. I sort through bundles of wooden stakes, pin flags, and rolls of orange tape in the back of the Suburban, setting aside his machete and his tattered Red Wing boots. After a thorough search up front, I find his leather wallet wedged between the two front seats where it blends in with the dark upholstery. Old age is a merciless bastard. But somehow, he's managed to stay in the mainstream, checking and signing off on surveys at the office of an old friend in Houston.

At noon, I unload the paint, lining the cans against a wall of the sun porch. Dad, already on his second Miller Lite, asks if I want one. While it's tempting, I open a diet drink instead, pouring it over ice.

"I got a call at the survey office the other day," he begins with a smile. "This woman said she thought there'd been a mistake on a survey I signed. Said the certification number of 563 was too *low*, that it should be in the *thousands*. So, I told her the number was correct, and she balked, asked me how I could be so sure. And I said, because it's *my* number." He chuckled and paused in reflection. "It would have been much lower if my boss hadn't stuffed my application into a drawer and forgotten about it."

I fell asleep that evening to the drone of the window units, thinking about how proud Dad is about his certification number, a number he'd lobbied for in Austin in the early 1950s before surveyors were certified. Then, sometime in the night, the window units cut off. Dad says a breaker kicked when both units cycled at the same time. The next morning, he wedges a Popsicle stick between the breakers and gets the juice flowing again before heading off to his new workshop to putter.

Dad had commissioned Kerry to build the workshop, and I watched the framing in during the Christmas holidays. Dad was the straw boss, an observer of young muscles doing the things he'd once done with little effort. After Ben and my nephews, Benjie and Taylor, got in on the action, their fluid motion reminded me of an impromptu outdoor ballet with Dad directing from the sidelines. More than a little sawdust is running through all their veins. Never content to sit and watch the world go by, after admiring Kerry's tool belt, Dad dashed off to the hardware store, my heart sinking a little when he came back with one of his own. That Kerry is carrying on the family tradition fills me with pride. There's no grass growing under his feet. Like Dad, he never stays idle for long.

Dad's been chomping at the bit to put Kerry to work on the old log cabin. The rough-hewn cedar logs of this hundred-year-old corn crib are still intact, but termites have eaten the insides from the rafters down. Kerry offers to help me move the furniture and paint the ceiling of the cabin before tackling the corn crib, so I'm up at 6:30 the next morning boxing up bottles, canned goods, and assorted junk. I hide a stack of wall calendars dating back to 1985, along with some tattered Texas stick flags that look like they've been here since Zapata left the area.

Dad's work clothes and barn jackets hanging in a corner go down in a heap of dust, and Kerry keeps finding cheese graters in every nook and cranny.

"What's Gramper doing with *five* cheese graters?"

I shrug my shoulders remembering the lost wallet as we uncover a lizard skeleton under the bureau and another wedged behind a switch plate. It seems that even in death, the "rusty guts" have the run of the place. I suppose the day will come when they'll own the cabin outright. Our discovery in no way hinders my determination to freshen it up with buckets of Laura Ashley Home paint, and we set to work.

While Kerry rolls the ceiling, we discuss the fire hazards as we uncover a maze of extension cords running in all directions. The stacked plugs remind me of the scene in *A Christmas Story* when Darren McGavin tries to plug in that hideous lamp and the sparks fly. Kerry wants to fill in every crack and hole with caulk and I keep reminding him that it's just a cabin, realizing that's the same thing my mother used to say to me.

I know we'll never get everything back the way it was. There's the intercom from Radio Shack that goes to the workshop, the extra loud ringer on the phone, the microwave, the toaster, the clock radio, and a task lamp over the dining table, to name but a few appliances hooked up to a network of cords.

After he leaves, I take a break on the porch. A radio station in Weimar is playing "When It's Polka Time in Texas," and I sit in my mother's wicker chair wondering if my heirs will ever know horned toads or mud daubers or what it's like to live with a mother who's clinically depressed. If Mom were here, she'd want to listen to anything by Willie Nelson. My family's taste in music was an eclectic mix. The first LP Dad brought home was an LP of his favorite waltzes by Johann Strauss.

Her first episode took place in the cabin on a Sunday while we were packing the car to leave. She started acting irrational, refusing to get in the car, then running to the big house, banging on the back door and sobbing to the tenants that Daddy was going to kill her. It was so off the wall we didn't know what to do, and poor Mrs. Roberts just stared at us with her mouth hanging open. I felt so sorry for Daddy that day, even sorrier for Mom.

The Blue Branch had been our safe haven for years. We'd even plotted our course there during the Cuban Missile Crisis. But on that particular day, not even the Blue Branch could soothe the beast within. Not long after that, Mom had a complete nervous breakdown.

I think it must have been during Mother's Blue Period, after she'd gone to a hospital in Providence for help with her depression, that we carried army cots down to the blue hole and spent the night under the stars. (I know we wouldn't have left her alone in the cabin, for she was deathly afraid of being alone at night.) Dad shielded his face with his hat as we bedded down, the white glare of the moon hitting us like a strobe. Later in the night, some of my grandfather's cattle wandered down to drink at the creek, bumping our cots like rude interlopers. Dad popped up from time to time to shoo them away, slapping at their rumps with his cowboy hat, but my zest for the outing soon waned as a screech owl cranked out its ghostly tremolo. Daddy liked to say we were "raised on concrete," two city kids who'd never studied by a kerosene lamp, or stuck a cow bloated on clover, watching the putrid gas rushing out of the cow's belly like a deflating tire. Although he always made us feel safe, protected from all harm, I didn't sleep a wink that night.

When the heat gets so oppressive we feel as if we're in equatorial Africa, Kerry runs down to the swimming hole for a quick dunk while I start a pot of chili on the apartment stove at Dad's request. The readings on the dials have worn off, and he's used a Magic Marker to note Hi, Med. and Lo. A nanosecond into my cooking, another breaker trips on what's shaping up to be a long week of Popsicle sticks. Late in the afternoon the four of us squeeze around the drop-down table for supper just like we've always done. Ben is scoping out the new paint job but says little, so it's hard to say what's on his mind. I can't dismiss the fact he and Dad are both Leos and butt heads on occasion. Or that Dad's current romantic entanglement has been eating at our nerves like a thousand tiny teeth.

It all started with Mother's death. Not right away, of course, but in phases, like opening a box and pulling out layers of tissue paper to see what lies beneath. I got just a glimmer of what might lie ahead the day we visited Stolz Memorials to pick out Mom's headstone. I'd been hounding Daddy about a stone for Mom's grave for months. Sonny Stolz and Dad had been school chums back in the 1930s, but Sonny had gone to Houston that day on business, so we were just wandering among the stones on display out front, sweltering in the hot Texas sun. As usual, Daddy was looking only at price while my brother and I wanted something grand, something in pink granite with carved flowers and flourishes and maybe a stone vase. I kept pointing to the double headstones and jotting notes in the penny notebook I always keep in my purse. I just assumed Daddy would want the double headstone. It made perfect sense to me. After all, they'd just celebrated their fifty-second wedding anniversary before Mom died. But when I pressed him about it, Daddy scratched his head and looked down at the Saint Augustine grass at our feet and said something to the effect, "What if I should remarry?"

Well, I felt like I'd been body-slammed. What if he *should* remarry, I remember thinking. Wouldn't he still want his final resting place with *Mother*? During a brief silence, my brother and I exchanged cursory glances. I guess we both knew right then that Daddy had a new paramour. A long pregnant pause ensued before we started looking at smaller, single stones. I was still holding out for a bouquet of flowers at the very least, but a modest unadorned stone won out, again because of price, and we agreed that Mom's epitaph would read *Loving Wife and Mother.* There was no denying that she was a loving person devoted to family, but a poem would have been nice, maybe something from Longfellow, one of her favorite poets. I'll never forget that day as long as I live, or all the days and months that followed. About a year later, I'd flown down for a visit to see the finished stone on Mom's grave. Prior to the visit, in one of our phone conversations, he said he'd had dinner with an old high school flame, and I could tell he was feeling me out. Of course I encouraged it. No man is an island. "I've been dating a *girl*," was the way he put it on our way to the airport. "And she's got a couple of kids."

I felt like a bomb had gone off in the car; it was just like him to tell me this at the last minute. And so off the cuff. What could I say? By the time we pulled into Passenger Pick-up I needed to pee, check my bag, and get my boarding pass, in that order! You *think you know somebody*. I wanted to like her. I wanted to believe it would work despite the age difference. Despite the constant news feeds about predators and the elderly. Despite the fact that the widowed father of a dear friend married a young woman and moved to Australia, only to come back penniless in less than a year, dragging his tail between his legs. I remember the dazed look on my friend's face that said there was nothing she could have done, no way to put out the fire.

You never think it's going to happen to you—until it does. I kept up a positive front, thinking there might be some potential there, some modicum of redemptive value, or that given enough time, the whole thing would fizzle out like a sparkler on the Fourth of July. Then we met Dad's girlfriend, and from that point on I dressed in full body armor, trying desperately to save Daddy and blot out the stain that kept spreading through the family like a dark blob of protoplasm.

She was slippery as an eel in hot oil, playing a disappearing act every time I came to town. When we finally managed to pin her down, I was horrified. Her head was about as empty as a box of Wheaties with the top blown off. I pictured the Anna Nicole Smith- J. Howard Marshall affair. Only Dad didn't have Marshall's millions. At some point he did admit to me that he'd misrepresented himself.

"She's a lot of fun," he'd said, waxing poetic, which explained his sudden interest in Pink Floyd when Willie Nelson had been the norm. I may as well have been talking to the Purple People Eater. I couldn't relate; wouldn't ever claim her as my stepmother if push came to shove. But after Daddy broke the ice about her existence and shattered life as we'd known it into a million tiny shards, he was ready to force each piece down our reluctant throats. What could they possibly have in common, I kept wondering. She didn't share Dad's enthusiasm for the ranch, or the outdoors in general, avoiding weekend trips there altogether. And she couldn't carry on an intelligent conversation with a toad. But it wasn't about that. It was about ego and loss and facing your own mortality. After Hurricane Katrina obliterated the city of New Orleans, the mayor said they'd lost their infrastructure. And I guess that's what happened to Daddy. After Mother died, he'd lost his infrastructure.

As the family scatters, I join Daddy on the porch for our quiet time together, dropping the window shade to block out the sun's orange glare just before sunset. Daddy's smoking a cigarette, his second of the day. After a lifetime of abstinence, he allows himself one with coffee in the morning and another in the evening. He appears to be in a meditative state, and I intervene by telling him I'd found Emil Dove, an old ranch hand listed in an old census at the Heritage Center, which sets off some kind of memory grenade.

"Emil's wife, Rosie used to chew up her food, then spit it into a spoon and feed it to their son Lonnie when he was a baby," Dad says, grinning "You remember Jack McLaughlin, one of our field hand? He lived over at the Munch place until it sold. And he had a little boy he called Butterbean. And whenever I saw them together, Jack would always say, 'Ivan looks just like his mama, don't he, Butterbean?'" Daddy snickers with this memory.

A train barrels past, setting off another grenade.

"You know, nobody knows this but me. But when Mom and Dad moved to Houston and Dad went to work for Hughes Tool, I never thought too much about it until one day I was talking to Mom on the phone. She said that Dad had been fired from the railroad. She confided that one day after he fired up the engine, he forgot to fill the steam boiler with water and the train stopped halfway between Houston and Corpus. She swore me to secrecy, but I guess she just needed to get that off her chest."

"And now you've gotten it off your chest," I smile. "It must have been a terrible humiliation for him, though, a real blow to his ego."

Dad stubs out his cigarette, thinking. He tells me about working for Otto Schnell at a hamburger stand in town.

"One night after my shift, he offered to drive me home. Well, as we were approaching the house, he stopped the car about halfway and doused the headlights. Then he put his arm around me and said he thought I was so cute he'd like to kiss me. I bolted from his car and hightailed it to the house, went straight to my room and never told my folks about it." "Good Lord! That's a lot of emotional baggage for a kid I said."

We sit in silence for a time, lost in our own thoughts when he tells me about his overnight with his grandmother Schaefer. "I was okay until it got dark. Then I got so homesick I started crying. I was sitting on the porch when Grandmother came up to me and pressed a silver dollar into my hand," he says, drifting off with a smile.

"One weekend in the 1940s, I drove to Monterrey, Mexico with some friends from A&M," he continued. "Outside of Monterrey we rented some donkeys to ride up to the top of Horsetail Falls. It was a desolate area and the trip was taking longer than we'd anticipated. We were getting pretty thirsty. Wondering if we should turn back. Then, just as we reached the top of the falls, there sat a bright red Coke machine." Dad chuckles at the memory.

One last memory grenade soon follows, about the time Dad and his younger brother Lelldon were duck hunting on the Trinity River. "One morning before daylight we were sitting in a blind and saw a guy waving a lantern from another boat off in the distance. We thought it might be a distress signal and rushed over to lend a hand. As soon as we pulled up alongside the other jon boat, this fisherman held up a big catfish he'd caught. He just couldn't wait to show it off."

After Daddy settles down in bed with his surveyor magazines, I step outside to take in the stars. They sparkle like diamonds on a clear night. I remember when the Milky Way and the Big Dipper filled the night sky like the poem: *Starlight/Star bright/First star I see tonight*. I return to the Blue Branch like a carrier pigeon that only knows one destination, while my widowed father returns each weekend to relive the halcyon days of his childhood. Like him, I come to stand in the firmament of my own youth, admire his vegetable garden, and drink in the solitude. But after he's gone, it's unclear just when I'll be back. I just don't know. ❧

Kerry and Yoshi at cabin (Author photo)

Chapter 12 – Surfside, Texas

Hope is forgetting that one's
Father will be in the deep, running currents
Forever

— THE PERSIMMON TREE CAROL, BY SHELBY STEPHENSON

In August of 2005, it was my son Kerry's idea to rent a beach house in August instead of spending a hot, sweaty week at the Blue Branch. I had some doubts about it at first, but after Dad put the *Sue-Ben* out to pasture and sold his other boats—first a twenty-foot Grady White, and later on, a twenty-three-foot Marathon with a head—we'd all gravitated to the ranch, and that has become our routine. Kerry's point was well taken. We needed a break from that routine. And I had to think long and hard to remember the last time we'd taken a family vacation at the beach. Weeks before the final arrangements were made, my brother phoned. The entire Texas coastline had been inundated with seaweed. While picturing our plans buried under great mounds of smelly, rotting Sargasso, I didn't let his grim report dampen my enthusiasm to revisit Surfside after a twenty-year absence. The seaweed turned out to be the least of my worries as I scheduled a root canal within days of my departure and stubbed my toe the night before my flight. I was gingerly slipping a sock over my blackened pinky early the next morning when an automated call came in from Northwest Airlines. My connecting flight had been cancelled at the last minute because there was no crew available, so I spent five hours in the Memphis airport drifting through shops filled with everything Elvis and eating airport fare. I toyed with the idea of catching a cab to Graceland, but thinking about the crime rate, I nixed the idea and pulled Cormac McCarthy's latest book, *No Country for Old Men*, from my carry-on, turning each page with deliberate slowness. Using an old snapshot from our last trip as a bookmark, I sat wondering if this beach thing was ever going to materialize. Then my cell phone rang. Kerry and my brother were on their way to Surfside wondering when I'd be there. I could practically taste the salt air on my tongue when Dad called from a surveyor's meeting, curious to know my whereabouts. I wished him a happy 85th birthday before boarding my connecting flight.

My friend Cathy—Ben's ex—and her husband, Steve, met me at Houston Intercontinental, their mini-van loaded with beach gear as I wedged my suitcase between chairs, umbrellas, and board games. I finally exhaled outside the city limits, remembering the puzzled looks from customers back in Raleigh when I spoke about my trip. Surfside, Texas, could have been another planet. To the uninitiated, Texas is a wind-scowled desert full of tumbleweeds and sage brush; they have no clue of its vast coastline teeming with bird life and estuaries from Port Arthur to Port Isabel. In my youth, I could have driven there blindfolded, but as we followed Highway 288 into Freeport, nothing looked familiar. Coasting through open country again, I told Steve to look for the massive Surfside Bridge that spans the Intracoastal Waterway, but we'd already crossed several bridges that fit that description. We'd passed fields of oil storage tanks, the Dow Chemical plant, and a sprawling refinery pumping the lifeblood of Texas through a network of pipes before I finally spotted the bridge.

If you suffer from any phobias, the Surfside Bridge will, quite literally, take your breath away. The decrepit old two-lane of my youth had been replaced by a new bridge that rises out of the earth like something prehistoric, and even with Steve at the wheel, my throat tightened up on our approach. I felt like we were creeping slowly to the top of the Texas Cyclone, the earth, sea, and sky all coming together at its crest. With the dunes and the breakers beckoning, I thought about the glory days surfing on long- boards with friends, picturing myself shagging barefooted across the concrete floor of a thatch-roofed Tiki bar. Never a place of grand hotels or fancy eateries, Surfside remains a small fishing village that never caught the eyes of developers. A Buc-ee's convenience store, a chain that would eventually envelop the state, had sprung up at the mouth of the bridge. Apparently, they saw the potential.

We hung a left on the Blue Water Highway, a beach road that runs along the dunes, a blur of cottages, palm trees and bait shops, coasting past a bar ditch full of salt cedars on one side, a salt marsh on the other. I took in the prairie of cord grass as far as the eye can see, ripe with the smell of pluff mud in the lowering tide. We drove the four miles of deserted beachfront, passing an abandoned fireworks stand and a deserted Perry's Convenience store (no relation) before pulling into the sandy drive of the white, stilted house at six o'clock. My frequent flyer miles had cost me dearly in time. The usual three-hour flight from Raleigh had taken twelve. Kerry and Ben were already in their bathing trunks unloading their short boards, and I cracked open a sweaty bottle of Corona Light and ran up the handicap ramp. To my relief, the seaweed had been scraped and piled against the dunes. I couldn't wait to feel the sand between my toes.

At some point, my nephews, Benjie and Taylor, showed up, and the house that started out as neat as a motel room soon turned into a clutter-fest of beach gear and bags, the quiet soon broken by a symphony of cell phones. Cathy's played "Alley Cat" and Steve's a Bach concerto. When I answered my chirping phone, Dad said he'd be there early the next morning. Standard seaside décor graced the walls of the living-dining area, and an oil painting of a cabin cruiser skimming the waves took me back to our days on the *Sue-Ben*. I picked a bedroom from the four available before returning to the kitchen, where I stuck a black-and-white photo of Mom and the original *Sue-Ben* on the fridge for old time's sake, thinking it really belonged in the Smithsonian instead of dry-rotting under a tarp at the ranch.

We lined our chairs across the front porch for happy hour and watched a string of pelicans as they cruised past, breaking formation to bob in the surf like loose-necked old men. The breeze coming off the Gulf was an aromatherapy unlike anything you might buy in a bath boutique, the sandy yard an explosion of Indian blanket and wild daisies. In the distance, cargo ships and oil tankers were lining up for clearance through the Intracoastal Waterway. As we watched local commerce in action, Cathy set out a generous supply of marinated shrimp to snack on. At some point we called it supper. Nobody felt like cooking or climbing back into the car to search for a restaurant. We were just too engaged by the shrimp boats dragging their nets through the warm waters of the Gulf and the fiddler crabs emerging at dusk and giving a neighborhood cat fits in the driveway below.

All my cares had long since melted away in the pounding surf until Dad arrived the next morning on the heels of my two nephews. While I helped him unload box after box of canned goods from his Suburban, he said, "Gee, you lifted that box like it was a feather." As I followed him up the handicap ramp thinking a strong gust might blow him over, I remembered a comment a friend's mother had made about her aging husband: "Why is it when men age, they forget how to *walk*?" Suddenly, all the humor had been dashed out of it like the crack from a bull whip. That he'd taken a week away from the office was highly unusual. Since his world is built around structure, he'd expressed concern that he wouldn't find enough to do on vacation. In days past, we'd spent every weekend on the *Sue-Ben*.

But he'd earmarked some local points of interest in a *Texas Parks and Wildlife* magazine, and we mapped out our week while Ben and the boys fished in the surf. Time moves forward faster than the speed of light. Twenty years ago, in my picture-turned-bookmark, my nephews had been little tykes more interested in building sand castles on the beach. Since school had started that week, we had the beach to ourselves. Cathy forgot to bring any reading material, so I handed her the McCarthy book with a warning: darker than the underbelly of a snake, but a page-turner. While I took short walks with Dad, picking up random shells and the occasional buckeye, it occurred to me I hadn't spent that much time one-on-one with any family member since our last beach vacation. At the ranch, everyone had their projects and scattered to the four winds until mealtime. As we took in the view, the sound of the surf set us adrift on a sea of remembrance. I recounted one of our early trips on the *Sue-Ben*. I'd reeled in a sizeable ling and just as it broke the surface, the line snapped. My heart sank right along with the big one that got away. During happy hour on the deck, my brother set out on his own voyage with stories I'd either forgotten or never heard before. I had only a foggy recollection of my cousin Gordon's salvage operation after a group of fishermen sank in a fifty-five-foot Hatteras about twenty-five miles out. With a fly deck and diesel engines, its value was roughly $300,000. The story going around some twenty years ago was this: These four guys were out fishing and drinking and inadvertently shut off the engines. The tubes began filling up slowly with water and they didn't notice the boat sinking until it was too late. They swam two miles to an offshore rig and clung to it until rescued. The Hatteras was sitting rightside-up about a hundred feet down with all the fishing poles still in place.

Using the inheritance Granddad left Gordon, he and Ben made about twenty trips out, once with a crew of divers, to salvage the boat. "I found the boat with a depth finder and dove right to it," Ben said, "but Gordon never had a good plan for raising the boat. And he wasn't open to other people's ideas." Cathy chimed in about the family dynamic, hinting that she knew several members of the Perry clan who could be equally as stubborn. On the last trip, they discovered the drums they'd positioned for floats and all the rods and reels had been taken, and they had no money left to continue the operation. At that point, Gordon's money had run out.

" One day I took some friends out in the Marathon," Dad grinned, "and we got caught in a bad storm, just blinding rain and rough seas all the way back. You couldn't see your hand in front of your face. I stuck my head inside the cabin to check on Bonnie, and there she was, putting on make-up. I asked her what in the world she was doing, and she said she wanted to look good when the Coast Guard found her body," he laughed.

Most days inside the Surfside house, Dad complained about the cold, getting blank stares all around as he said, "Shiver me timbers. It's cold in here." Most nights, after everyone had gone to bed, with my brother snoring in the next room, I'd hear Dad shuffling down the hallway to the thermostat, turning the dial until the AC unit shut off before he shuffled back to bed, getting his sweet revenge. One of our daily pastimes was using an old set of binoculars Dad had bought with S&H green stamps to watch an offshore rig coming together. While crew boats hauled supplies back and forth and helicopters shuttled workers from rig to shore, a standby boat at the ready in case of a blowout, Dad recounted the day he'd taken a crew boat from Freeport to position a rig for Amoco, only to discover the rig hadn't shown up. "The crew boat didn't have a galley, and after we ate our sandwiches, we rode around until it started getting late. We pulled alongside a barge, and I recognized a friend of mine, Clyde Thompson, grilling steaks. I said, 'Boy, those steaks smell mighty good,' and Clyde invited me aboard for supper. I spent the night on the barge instead of going back to the motel in Freeport. Amoco didn't make a fuss about it," he smiled. "They still paid for my motel room."

I took a break from inactivity on the porch to check my cell phone, surprised to find a voicemail from a childhood friend from the old neighborhood. My immediate thought was that there'd been a death in the family, but when I returned Richard's call, he said he just wanted to ask Ben something. It sounded so mysterious that I relayed the message to Ben when he got back from his beer and ice run. (The weekend wasn't over yet, and already I wondered how we ever got along without cell phones.) After Ben dumped another twelve-pack of Bud Light into the cooler, he disappeared for a time, then stood on the porch surveying the beach. I can't always read him and he's not always forthcoming with information. Like any red-blooded woman, I wanted to hear the dirt. After dropping a few hints, he spoke in a tone somewhere between amusement and disgust.

"Richard wants his Channon board back." He fell into stony silence and I read between the lines, remembering the surfing trip at Sergeant Beach back in the 1960s that more or less wrecked their friendship. Ben was riding on top of the family station wagon looking for waves while Richard, driving at a snail's pace, suddenly gunned the car forward, traveling across a washboard of sand at high speed before hitting the brakes. Ben flew off the roof and landed on the hood, grabbing the windshield wipers, which promptly snapped off. Wiper blade in hand, he was thrown off the car, hitting the packed sand with such force he broke a number of bones including his arm and leg. The surfboard, now a collector's item, had been Richard's peace offering at the time.

"And you're *not* giving it back," I mused. "I said I'd trade it for Arthur's .455 Webley & Scott from the war but his wife wouldn't allow it," Ben said. He threw his head back and laughed wickedly before stomping off to the beach. The timing of the call was uncanny. It was as if the long arm of collective consciousness had reached down from the heavens and thumped Richard's head, screaming, *Your Channon board has come out of hiding. It's at Surfside Beach. Do not hesitate. Make your move now.* It was something else to ponder during my idle hours on the porch.

On Monday, Dad started going down a list of charter boats and making calls. Though a big party boat cost eighty dollars a head, complete with a comfortable air-conditioned lounge that served food and beverages, he really preferred a private charter. We coughed at the going rate, about one-fifty a head, but we wanted to give him a special birthday. He reserved a boat for Wednesday and, after lunch, a yard maintenance crew appeared, cranked up a riding lawnmower and a trimmer, and began mowing down all the pretty wildflowers around the house. Cathy and I were livid, but hated to stir up any bad blood. Then Dad left for the marina to check out the charter boat. "Enjoy your peace and quiet," he laughed on his way down the ramp, returning an hour later in total disgust. The boat was a forty-year-old rust bucket unfit for man or beast; no way he'd set foot on a boat with the name *Nightmare*. He cancelled the reservation and got back on the phone.

The next charter boat Dad inspected passed muster, so early on Wednesday morning we loaded ice chests with sandwiches, beer, water, and soft drinks before setting out for the marina at 6 o'clock. There was a six-person limit, and since Steve is prone to getting seasick, he and Cathy bowed out. Our Captain, David Smith, didn't take credit cards, so I was short on cash. Like a true sister, Cathy loaned me some money and said she'd be content to stick around the house and cook all day. In return, I promised to take lots of pictures.

The *Rock Bottom* was a clean, forty-six-foot lobster boat with a fly deck and two large fish coolers full of ice on the main deck; all the bait and tackle was provided. I recounted the cash under the dim light of a vapor lamp before handing it to Captain Smith, who said it was customary to wait until the end of the trip to pay. I don't know what bothered me most, being called "ma'am" or making a gaff so early on, but I'd no sooner stuffed the wad of bills and personal checks into my bag when I noticed a sign inside the cabin that read: *Your crew works hard. Tips are appreciated. Fish Cleaning is Extra.* Before firing up the Cummings twin-diesel engines, Captain Smith introduced us to his father, our one-man crew for the day, as we rumbled through the Intercoastal waterway, passing an abandoned jack-up rig and the Surfside jetties on our way out.

The sun was just beginning to show itself when my thoughts turned to all those early mornings on the *Sue-Ben* with Dad at the helm. Sometimes we'd drop anchor near a deserted beach and wade ashore with a picnic basket. Salami sandwiches on pumpernickel bread were standard fare, but sometimes we'd gather drift wood and roast weenies. Though I'll always remember those days with sheer bliss, seeing the man who'd been our polestar sitting idle on a bunk in a strange boat was like hitting all the wrong keys on a piano, the notes distorted and brash. On the other hand, I'd certainly forgotten how breathtaking a sunrise can be out on the Gulf. The horizon reminded me of a moody pastel with broad brush strokes of indigo and ever-changing layers of soft grays and pinks that disappeared like vapor trails in the rising sun. I felt no urgency about the squall miles behind us. Cloudbursts had been drifting all around the beach house since our arrival.

After the sun came up, we caught the fullness of its glare, and Dad realized he'd forgotten his sunglasses. Thankfully, Mr. Smith Sr. loaned him a pair. We hadn't really had a calm day since our arrival. Though this day promised to be a good one, there was still enough wave action to keep us on our toes. Dad said, "Keep your eyes on the horizon and you're not as apt to get seasick." But in all the years we've been out together, I've never been seasick. Maybe he'd forgotten. Dad kept teetering every time he stepped out onto the deck and I worried he might fall overboard. When he eyed the fly deck and started to climb the steep ladder, I grabbed the back of his belt and held on. I guess he thought better of it as we tied up to Brazos 417, a production rig some ten miles out. The first mate baited our jigs with herring while a dull fog horn on the platform sounded every few seconds. Ben used to snorkel and spearfish, but I never got into the sport. Ever the ninny, I always worried about sharks, giant manta rays, and other denizens of the deep. The old rig reminded me of Ben's narrative about Cathy's father, Admiral Taylor. A group of Navy Seals had invited Admiral Taylor to join them on a training mission at the Flower Garden Banks, a National Marine Sanctuary and coral reef 100 miles off the Galveston coast. Another boat picked up the Admiral and a few divers later, and as they were heading back to shore, they stopped at an abandoned rig to do a little spear fishing. One of the divers jumped in before anybody was ready. After the man speared a large Jewfish using steel cable, the huge fish circled around him, pinning him to the legs of the rig where he drowned. He'd broken the first rule: Never dive alone. A pair of wire cutters or shared oxygen tank would have saved him.

With nothing but small sharks striking our jigs, we moved on. Fifteen miles out, the water turned from a murky grayish-green to a brilliant turquoise that flickered and danced off the ceiling of the cabin. We tied up to a platform that screeched like an owl from a speaker high up, a warning to boats navigating at night or in a fog. This spot proved to be more productive, though I felt like a pin ball out on the deck. As the boat kept rhythm with the rolling water, Dad got comfortable sitting on an ice chest, holding his line over the side. He seemed to be enjoying himself in a slow, methodical kind of way, but it saddened me to think he's outlived all his fishing buddies. After the boys started pulling up red snapper hand over fist, I decided to get in on the action and got a good strike on my first cast. With my adrenalin pumping, it took everything I had to reel in what felt like Orca the killer whale at the other end. Cussing like a sailor, my muscles screaming, my fish finally broke the surface. I'd landed another ling. This one didn't get away, but at thirty inches, it wasn't a keeper. I handed Kerry my camera. At the very least, I wanted a picture before the first mate tossed it overboard. It seemed we were reliving our seafaring history together. The only thing missing was our mother.

After the breeze died, the deck felt like the inside of a kiln. We passed a gallon jug of water around and ate our sandwiches while moving further out to fish for king mackerel, drifting behind the *Angelina*, a weather-beaten white shrimp boat from Houston. I'd never been that close to a shrimp boat at sea before; the lines on the mast were alive with gulls that sounded like canned laughter above the drone of the diesel engines. The captain and crew looked like rough customers straight out of *Treasure Island*, making me uneasy as I recalled the brutal war that broke out after Vietnamese shrimpers began competing with Texas shrimpers in the Gulf of Mexico, depleting the waters of the bays months after the Vietnam War ended. The fished-out waters of Galveston Bay could have been the Dead Sea in the aftermath; Dad's own short-lived shrimping expeditions were never as fruitful as they'd been in the past. Before I could say "Sixteen men on a dead man's chest," we were moving on again. And yo-ho-ho and a bottle of rum, I was relieved.

In early afternoon, we idled behind a black shrimp boat out of Tampa called the *Captain Raleigh*. I made a remark about the name coincidence, but the guys were all sweat and muscle, too busy bending and reeling like a set of bobble-head dolls to make the connection. At twenty miles out, the water changed color again and we floated on a rhapsody of cobalt blue. While our captain tossed out chum, a pod of bottlenose dolphins attracted to the mackerel circled our boat in an undulating ballet, one of those magical moments I'd lost touch with. As a mother and her calf surfaced side-by-side, I thought about what a living, breathing entity the Gulf really is, and how it used to be our second skin. Though Dad had grown restless to head back, it was hard for the rest of us to call it a day and say goodbye to Mother Ocean. We fell silent during the two- hour trip back to Surfside. Lost in my own thoughts, I wondered if Dad found our outing somewhat bittersweet.

Great orange rafts of Sargasso stood out like neon against the deep blue water as I stood on the deck with the salt air whipping through my hair, waving to the occasional boat and clinging tenaciously to our old life. I saw my brother's reflection in the water before the salt-and-pepper hair came, Dad's when he still had thick dark hair slicked down with Brylcreem, his back stick- straight. I saw myself on the foredeck of the *Sue-Ben*, dressed in a frilly swimsuit, my hair in a ponytail, Mother inside the cabin smoking a "cig." There'll always be a part of us out there in the ether where I'm reeling in that giant ling.

I stepped off the boat and onto the dock on sea legs. I hadn't felt that rubbery, rocking sensation for a long time, and joined Dad and some locals under a small shed, reliving our day while Ben and Mr. Smith Sr.

cleaned our catch. Supper would be late. Foodie that I am, I'd packed a two-pound bag of House Autry seafood breader for the trip and looked forward to the fish-fry to come. I discreetly took up a collection of tip money, so much the wiser at the end of the day.

Thursday was our last full day at the beach and we decided to soak it all in. Cathy wanted to explore High Island, but Steve's back had gone out and he was laid up on the futon. We'd hardly put a dent in the industrial-sized can of Wolf Brand Chili Ben brought, so I made one last bowl of Frito pie for lunch. After Ben and the kids scattered to San Luis Pass to fish along the salt marsh, Dad and I explored old Surfside Village, a community lean on plantings and big on wide open spaces of St. Augustine grass, a neighborhood as flat as a pool table.

Creeping along the grid of narrow streets, I crooked my head inconspicuously out the window and snapped a picture of a salt-blown cabin draped in fish netting.

"Stop at the one shaped like a lighthouse," I motioned, "the one with the old cannon in the yard."

We passed a brown geodesic dome and a white cottage with cutwork deck railings of bright yellow sunbursts—quaint little reminders of a yesterday that's gone untouched. If only life could be as simple as this little fishing village and stay just the same. In an era of development from coast to coast, it seemed unprecedented that Surfside hadn't changed one iota.

Aside from a stingray that popped Ben on the ankle and a seatbelt violation Kerry had to deal with, there'd been no real mishaps all week. No undertow, no invasion of men-of-war or slimy jellyfish. There had been some reports of isolated shark attacks further up the coast, but I wanted one good swim on my last day and invited Dad to join me late in the afternoon.

"This is the first time I've worn these bathing trunks in over ten years," he said as we lugged two beach chairs over the dunes. We watched a sandpiper hobble around on little twig feet, skirting the incoming foam as we lathered sunscreen on our shoulders and stepped into surf as warm as bathwater. "Remember how we used to call it suntan lotion?" I shouted. But he couldn't hear me over the thundering surf. The waves got pushy before we were even waist deep, and I jumped at every clump of Sargasso that pricked my legs. After Dad teeter-tottered, I grabbed his hand and held on tight, wading back in tide-and-time, no longer the little girl in the inner tube, but the frightened "parent" worried the next wave might knock him down with a one-two punch.

On our last day, I sat on the deck visiting with Dad while everybody packed up. The plan was that after Kerry dropped me at the airport, he'd join Dad, Ben, and my nephews at the Blue Branch for the weekend. Dad wasn't happy about my leaving and didn't understand why I wasn't coming with them to the ranch. And when I tried to explain, he broke down in great heaving sobs that drew everybody out to the deck to see what was wrong.

"He's just seen his mortality," Cathy whispered as I ran into the house for some tissues. It was one of those pivotal moments I wish I could do over again: rebook my flight and drive to the ranch with Dad.

Later that month, Hurricane Katrina made landfall near New Orleans. I watched in horror as helicopters rescued those stranded on rooftops after the levees failed. Then, on the heels of Katrina, Hurricane Rita, a Category 5 storm, had me reeling as it made a bee-line for Houston. I shouldn't have been surprised by either storm. The Gulf waters had been unusually warm that first week of August. With Katrina fresh on everyone's mind, all of Houston, it seemed, had started evacuating the city. Even Houston's mayor urged everyone to leave, telling residents, "Don't wait. The time for waiting is over."

When I phoned Dad to see what precautions he'd taken, he said he was heading for the Blue Branch. Little did we know that he'd be driving right into a nightmare: the largest evacuation in U.S. history and the worst gridlock Houstonians had ever endured as three million people packed up and headed out of town. But Dad was one of the lucky ones. It only took him the better part of the day, in bumper-to-bumper traffic, with his faithful companion, Princess, by his side, to get from Highway 6 to 290, and on to La Grange, a trip that normally takes about an hour. And he talked about it later as if it were just another adventure among the many he's had during his lifetime. ❧

Left to Right: Daddy, me, nephews Benjie and Taylor and brother Ben on the Rock Bottom

Chapter 13 – Have You Ever Been To Texas In The Spring?

Meadows… filled with wildflowers the color of your mother's eyes.
Horizons that go on and on—dizzying you the way the hills of Georgia,
Alabama and the Carolinas never could.

— TEXAS POETRY CALENDAR 2015 BY MARGARET DORNAUS

The mild, sunny days of spring are the most enjoyable ones to visit the Blue Branch, and my internal clock is set for the first week in April, when the wildflower season is in full swing across the Texas Hill Country. I pack for the spring showers that will require a raincoat, the cold front that invariably blows in from the north, chilling us to the bone, or the warmer days that will have me reaching for my shorts.

If the rains are plentiful through the winter months, bluebonnets will coat the countryside in shades of cerulean and cobalt blue, the oils gently squeezed and mixed as on an artist's palette. I'll look for the less obvious flowers of the wild verbena and the wine cups that stand out like neon lights along the fence lines and might turn the most steadfast agnostic into a believer.

As the state bursts at the seams with this springtime renewal, tour buses will wheeze along the backcountry roads from Brenham to San Antonio, carrying tourists from ranch to ranch to view crimson fields of Texas paintbrush, a scattering of prickly white poppies, or evening primroses lying in wait just around the next bend. The Texas bluebonnet (*lupinus texensis*) is what they come for. And to capture this ever-changing canvas of blues and pinks and reds, a mother or father will park the family wagon alongside the road and pose, or snap a few pictures of an especially brilliant hillside while the kids scatter to pick a bouquet.

Twelve years after my mother's death, having put his Bear Creek house on the market, my father has taken up permanent residence in the cabin, downsizing from three bedrooms to a small space without closets. It wasn't supposed to be this way, but he's fallen on hard times. No choice in the matter. At present, he's living the simple life of a country gentleman and doesn't seem bothered by his financial downfall.

The fleece pull-over my brother sent me for Christmas, a flattering shade of powder blue, feels just right against the morning chill. Blue for the Blue Branch, I wonder? Or for the bluebonnets? I think something has crawled under the cabin and died since my last visit. The odor, somewhere between the smell of boiled cabbage and wet dog, is an assault on the senses. I open some of the jalousies on the porch to let in the fresh air and a few mud- daubers drift in. There are no screens because Dad says they muddy the view, an argument Mother and I gave up on long ago.

I'm here to help Dad get organized. My friend Kay is coming from Houston to lend a hand, but our dear friend Fritzeen couldn't make it this year. Since moving her elderly mother from Lubbock out to her home in California, it's become harder for her to get away for our spring reunions. I try not to think about how much I'll miss her, turning my attention to the need for some room freshener. I'll pick some up at the Dollar General later.

Henry David Thoreau said that in a pleasant spring morning, all sins are forgiven. With that in mind, I'm not going to dwell on the fact that my father got involved with a young woman (young meaning my son's age) who fleeced him of all his money, or that he owes back taxes to the IRS, or that the engine of his Suburban blew up at 300,000 miles and he can't afford to replace it. I'm not going to grumble about the soft housing market or the foreclosure notice that came in the mail, or the money I wired him last Father's Day to cover his overdrafts. I'm not going to make a judgment call on the loneliness of an old man, or revisit the guilt of not being around to protect him from himself. I had thought fleetingly of picking up the tab on his mortgage, but decided it would surely be financial suicide, and, besides, like any good game of chess, my dad's money troubles forced the Houston hussy to move out. (Not that she's forgotten how to use the telephone.)

He knows he's welcome to come live with us in North Carolina, but he'd rather wrestle a bobcat barehanded than leave Texas. He's like the worm inside an apple. To the worm, the whole world is an apple. And Dad's world has always been Texas and the Blue Branch. He seems content with his Social Security and pension but he wants to, *needs* to, keep his hand in the business of surveying, content to drive the little Ranger pickup he bought for a song ten years back.

It isn't unusual for my father's life to be riddled with complications—some so complex a genie couldn't figure them out. But I won't turn my back on a man who's sweet as Tupelo honey; the father who told us countless bedtime stories about his life at the Blue Branch; the man who stood by as our mother struggled with depression when a lesser man would have bailed. He's every bit the "gentle man" my grandfather was, and together, they put the word *gentle* in gentleman. He never spanked me or Ben, and only raised his voice to me twice in my girlhood, the first time when I brought home a 45 RPM of a hit song, "Keep A-Knockin." I'd saved my allowance to get it and couldn't contain my excitement as I set it on the turntable of our stereo. But as soon as Little Richard started wailing like a man on fire, Daddy set off his own firestorm, his bigoted side coming through: "No daughter of mine is going to keep a record like that in this house!"

The second time, he put his foot down about my attending a co-ed pajama party in high school. It was my senior year, with rounds and rounds of parties, all featuring entertainment by popular bands. Bobby "Blue" Bland was scheduled to appear at this one, and I wouldn't have missed it if St. Peter came down from the heavens and confronted me himself. I threw a hissy fit, but it didn't sway Dad one bit. Though I'd dutifully returned Little Richard to the corner grocery store back in 1957, I did manage to sneak out to the pajama party after my beau and I set up the caper. He'd pick me up dressed in street clothes, and I'd sneak my pajamas out of the house in my oversized bag, changing clothes at a local gas station. We pulled it off without a hitch, no real harm done, Dad none the wiser for it.

The cluttered porch has become his new headquarters, made even smaller by the addition of another filing cabinet and an exercise bike. I can remember not so many years ago, he built the new workshop to take some of the load from the cabin. But now everything has been reversed; the workshop is now a storage unit for the family furniture we didn't want to part with. The cabin is long overdue for an upgrade. The plastic shower stall is stained and brittle, and the settings have worn away from the dials on the apartment stove again, a stove covered in grease splatters so thick it might take a blow torch to remove them.

Dad has added a fax machine to the drop-down table, a meager space to begin with, and hopes Kay will help him figure out how to use it. The blizzard of papers, unopened mail, and bills scattered across the room are unwelcome interlopers. Add to that the minefield of cardboard filing boxes and an explosion of garbage bags that hold who knows what, and the cabin feels more like a toxic landfill than the quaint little getaway I remember.

I don't think this is going to go down as one of the more memorable spring visits I've had. Texas is experiencing an extreme drought, the wildflowers scarce as hen's teeth. By mid-morning I've usually picked several bouquets of flowers and set them around the cabin, but I've lost my enthusiasm for it. Dad says that a month or two ago my brother ran over the pole outside with the tractor, shattering the plantation bell into a hundred pieces. Ben said it was an accident. Said it with the nonchalant attitude of someone who'd just run over an ant hill. Dad says he's really pissed about it and doesn't see how it was an accident. I'm not getting involved.

After a brief search for the remote, I set the big-screen TV jammed behind the entry door to a musical station, beginning with "Traditional

Jazz" to get the day started. I'm cleaning coffee stains from the sink when I see Kay's white Toyota pulling around the sweep of gravel before she parks under the Perry Oak.

"Where's the plantation bell?" she asks as soon as she's inside.

We sigh, explaining the situation in the vague sort of way you'd tell a toddler her puppy got run over by the lawnmower. I can see her mind processing the information before she says "Okay," drawing the word out in contemplation before moving on. Kay and I go back thirty-plus years. She's taken early retirement, first from her birddog position as a criminal prosecutor for Harris County, most recently from private practice after winning some big judgments. When we first met, she carried a floppy canvas bag around town that read: *A Woman's Place is in the House and the Senate*. That she ran for a judgeship and lost bothers me to this day. She would have made an excellent judge in a courthouse that once reeked of corruption and malfeasance.

If I were describing Kay to a stranger, I'd say she could charm the fillings right out of al-Qaida's back teeth. Free from the shackles of litigation, she enjoys island-hopping in the Caribbean with her sister and brother-in-law, living on island time aboard their sailboat, the *Cloud 9*. She has a close kinship with my dad, as excited about spending a weekend in the cabin with us as she is about sailing from the island of Bonaire to Trinidad.

It's hard to look at Kay without thinking about Fritzeen during our salad days when we were a threesome always looking for Mr. Right or some far-flung adventure. In the spring of 1981, the three of us flew to Cancun with my son, Kerry, and Fritzeen's son, J. Scott, catching a Mexican passenger ferry to *Isla de la Mujeres*, the Island of Women. I had my doubts about the condition of the ferry boat, but Kay was old world about such things and, putting our trust in her, we boarded. I can still picture her sitting on the dock in her floppy straw hat and espadrilles, casually thumbing through a travel brochure without a care in the world. This wasn't her first trip to the island, and she waxed poetic about her deep dive to some underwater caves to view the sleeping sharks. The sea is a wilderness experience I only relish from the safe vantage point of the shoreline, or from a comfortable, seaworthy boat. Two days later, I snapped her picture swimming with the sea turtles near the shoreline.

We checked in to a quaint hotel at Isla Mujeres, our rooms overlooking a picture post card of turquoise water, white sand, and thatched huts where the locals slept in net hammocks to stay cool and avoid snakes. After three days of communing with the iguanas, catching a Mexican circus, shopping for peasant dresses, and watching the windsurfers gliding in from Cancun over Margaritas each afternoon, at Kay's prodding, which met with some resistance from Fritzeen, we left our little Caribbean paradise, returning to the mainland, where we piled into a rented VW Beetle bound for the Mayan ruins of Chichen Itza. Ordinarily, I'm the designated driver, but I felt a twinge of *tourista* coming on, Kay and Fritzeen having polished off the bottle of Pepto Bismol I'd brought. So I turned the wheel over to Kay thinking, What's the worst that could happen?

The roads through the jungle of the Yucatan were thick and menacing, a tropical rain forest of rubber trees big as oaks and croton plants approaching the size of modest houses. Since I'd started a tropical plant business some years before, the sight of these ordinary house plants growing into behemoths in their natural habitat was mind boggling but hard to enjoy while bumping around in the back seat with the boys, sipping bottled water and fighting nausea. While the steamy-jungle air drafted through the windows like a blast furnace, I wasn't sure if we were driving through paradise or purgatory. Now and again the jungle opened up into large areas of slash-and-burn, still smoldering where a tangle of vines and every other living thing threatened encroachment. We hadn't seen a cantina or another car for hours when we spotted two *mestizos*, Spanish for mixed-race, in the road up ahead, waving at us moronically. I thought, well, here we are. Three single women with two small boys in tow, out here in the middle of nowhere, and me, weak as a kitten. Jesus H. Christ, we ought to have our heads examined.

Kay crept to a standstill, and we were going over our options as the pair approached the car, all smiles, two small men with dirty bandanas wrapped around their heads. If anybody can get us out of this, I thought, I suppose it will be Kay. But our Spanish did us no good, for these men of the jungle spoke some dialect we couldn't make out. I soon forgot about my bellyache when a loud explosion threw dirt and debris in all directions from a ditch up ahead. As soon as they gave us the all-clear, waving us on, Kay hit the gas with a vengeance and we all heaved a collective sigh of relief as we sped through the jungle. I guess God and good luck were with us that day. The two workers we'd been so wary of had been setting off dynamite to clear the road. We were driving in silence, collecting our thoughts, when Fritzeen started giggling. It wasn't long before Kay and I followed suit, thinking about what could have been while trying to come down from a bone-rattling adrenalin rush.

Late in the afternoon, and road weary, we checked into the Hacienda Chichen, a charming 17th century colonial on the outskirts of the ruins where the jungle had been carefully harnessed, trimmed, and restrained.

The hacienda was a tropical Eden, lush with well-tended gardens and fountains, and trees bursting with bromeliads. The boys soon appeared in their swim trunks, picking fresh limes from the surrounding bushes before doing belly-flops and back-flips into the pool. By late afternoon I was feeling human again and we dressed for supper, walking to the open-air restaurant where our table on the patio looked out over great clumps of variegated ginger in full bloom, along with a tree the locals called a golden chain for its bright-yellow streamers cascading to the ground.

The place reeked with atmosphere from the starched linen tablecloths to the vases of bright red bougainvillea on each table. We ordered baked ham and fresh pineapple with mango chutney sauce, and Kay gave me one of her broad, toothy grins and said, "I told you this would be fun." While we waited for our meal, she was already in full swing, going on to explain that "chi" means mouth in Mayan, and "chen" means well, therefore the site means "mouth of the well." "Itza" was the branch of the Mayan tribe that settled there.

As the ruins beckoned, with their ancient ball courts, serpentine temples, and sacrificial wells, and with Kay wondering aloud if we could squeeze in a trip to Merida before our plane left Cancun, the ice-cold bottle of Tecate the waiter brought me never tasted so damned good.

"Where'd you get the exercise bike?" Kay asks in her usual upbeat, gleeful voice, climbing onto the seat and manning the controls. The computerized screen with various settings that measure distance and difficulty is something Dad's been unable to master.

"I still haven't figured out how to work the thing," Dad says as Kay begins to pedal. "It's just like riding a bike, but it's *real* hard to turn," he chuckles.

While Dad and Kay study the instruction manual for the fax machine, I get busy stripping the beds. "When's the last time your sheets were washed?" I ask in passing.

"When's the last time you were here?" Dad grins, as I carry a bundle out to the big house. As far as I can tell, the only thing that won't require cleaning is the small chest freezer. Because he was late paying the electric bill last month, the power was cut off. The rest goes without saying.

After I start the wash, Jim Kiger, a friend from the neighboring ranch, comes rolling in on his Alligator to say hello and chat. He and his wife live on the other side of the creek on a piece of land my grandparents sold to the Munch family to make it through the Depression. After Jim retired from his machine shop in Houston, he and Mary bought the property from the Munch heirs. They used to host a big shindig every July Fourth with all the barbecue brisket you could eat and beer you could drink, along with an impromptu happy hour every Friday evening for close friends.

Dad always looked forward to Fridays at their "Pastime Club," but in recent years, Jim's had some health problems and had to quit the boozing and partying. He's a fun-loving, salt-of-the-earth kind of guy with an unruly crop of white hair and fair skin. He and Mary have spent a small fortune on their sprawling brick ranch house, adding a three-bedroom guest house, and most recently, a spacious bunk house with all the trappings. If they get bored, they'll go out and buy a windmill or a hot tub, or order a custom entry gate, or build a pond or install a grape arbor or an outdoor kitchen, or purchase a prized bull to add the ever-expanding herd of cattle they never tire of talking about. In contrast, their place makes ours look like a shantytown. Jim chats with Dad about controlling fire ants and the prospect of making enough hay for his cattle this year what with the drought, but I suspect the Kigers will muddle through somehow.

While Dad gets back to the meets-and-bounds he'd been working on, composing a description of a property Ben had surveyed, Kay tackles the oven and I make a hasty trip to Dollar General for more cleaning supplies. After lunch, Dad pulls a ball cap from his collection, the one from the Mule Days Festival in Benson, North Carolina, where I live, and we walk out to the vegetable garden to see what's been planted and what's growing. Like Jim Kiger, Dad has had his own health issues over the years, starting with a hip fracture after Mom died, black-outs that required a pacemaker, and more recently, osteoarthritis that has him bent over like a pretzel when he walks. It's hard to look at him and remember the man who once rode horseback across the dunes of High Island while surveying for Amoco, heeler dogs in tow tracking rattlesnakes and breaking them in two with a few swift jerks. Kay has always shared Dad's enthusiasm for gardening, never hesitating to pitch in. But today, the vegetables are a brief respite from cleaning. We walk the rutted and cracked rows, admiring his tomato plants, string beans, and corn. He points to a row of okra at the far end, grabbing the water hose to irrigate. His fruit orchard needs mowing, and when he says he might get around to it later, depending on his back, Kay makes the comment that every gardener needs a cast iron back with a hinge. They chuckle in unison.

We drive out to the front gate where one nice stand of bluebonnets and paintbrush are blooming in a low area that apparently holds moisture. We snap a few pictures together, knowing this will be the extent of our wildflower expeditions this year. At five o'clock, I yell out that my get-up-and-go just got up and went and Kay says my headstone should include a picture of a jug of Clorox. She's about to get the last of the penicillin cleaned out of the mini-fridge. When she hollers, "Oh my God!" Dad raises his voice from the porch, "If it walks out on its own, kill it."

I change the station to "Acoustic Crossroads an eclectic blend of alt-country and bluegrass that doesn't seem to offend anybody. The small luxury of music makes the day feel brighter, though Richard and Linda Thompson's melancholy rendition of "Dimming of the Day" sets my heart on edge. After I hand Dad a Miller Lite and crack open two bottles of Corona, he starts to say something, then hesitates as the blast from a whistle signals an approaching train. After the rolling thunder of the engine and the screech of empty coal cars braking stops, he says my brother is grilling doves for supper and asked if I'd make some potato salad. Ben also wanted to know if we had any toothpicks.

"What does he need with toothpicks?" Dad wonders. "Are they to pick our teeth with after supper?"

After I explain they're for securing the bacon he'll wrap around the doves for grilling, we all share a hearty laugh. Kay has the apartment stove gleaming again and even marked the controls using a black Magic Marker, which feels like a small miracle as I set a burner on high and start a pot of water boiling for the eggs. We clear all the files from Dad's work table and eat supper on paper plates on the porch because my brother gutted the kitchen in the big house for remodeling two years ago. With the exception of the oven—he moved the fridge into the dining room—it's still sitting empty and forlorn. Ben says he has big plans for the remake, which include tile floors and cherry cabinets. Dad says under his breath that he hopes he lives to see it. After supper we clear the table, returning all of Dad's files, pens, rulers, and notebooks to their approximate positions. When Kay heads for the shower, I remind her that the hot and cold knobs are reversed so she won't accidentally scald herself. Dad turns on the task light that's suspended from the ceiling on two chains and gets back to one of his surveys. He says this one's complicated because of so many heirs to the property. I close the jalousies, but a few moths slip in anyway, hovering near the task light in an orgasmic rage and clearing out the dust motes we missed earlier.

The birds begin to stir at daybreak, first a cardinal, then a bob white and later a wren, until they make up a chorus outside my window. Half-awake, I smell coffee brewing and know I'll have to get up when another train comes crashing through our peace and quiet, shaking the cabin as though an earthquake is upon us. Dressed in a fresh white shirt and khaki pants, Dad walks in carrying a newspaper and a box of sticky buns from Lukas Bakery, complaining he can't find a *Houston Chronicle* in town anymore, only the Austin paper. We're all addicted to the local paper, a throwback to a time when that's the only news there was. It's a typical spring morning in central Texas, a dense fog blotting out the sun like a curtain of batting. Just when you think you'll never see blue sky again, it burns off around mid-day.

The comforting aroma of yeast and cinnamon fill the cabin as we dig into the sticky buns and pour coffee into Styrofoam cups. Before Kay packs to leave, she puts on her red-white-and-blue ADA ball cap from her years as Assistant District Attorney and we hike down to the lower pasture, walking once around the loop for old time's sake. The Austin bypass has added a new layer of noise I find irritating, but it doesn't seem to bother Kay as we pass one of my brother's deer blinds and a few anemic patches of bluebonnets, remembering years when the pasture looked like a shag carpet of royal blue and the fence lines were thick with wine cups and pink primroses.

She hasn't complained about the lumpy mattress, and I wish I could join her in Houston and sit around her pool drinking margaritas like in the old days. Instead, we talk about the issues of aging parents (she lost hers two years ago), living wills, and the eventuality of letting go. I tell her that Dad's only major complaint about moving to the Blue Branch is that he doesn't know where to meet any women. "Where's the Chicken Ranch when you *really* need it?" she chuckles.

The afternoon is uneventful, more organizing and toting boxes of file folders to the workshop. Dad decides to take a break from his survey to hoe some weeds in his garden, picking through an array of misshapen and sweat-stained ball caps hanging on the wall above the freezer. I caution him not to overdo it while putting together some tuna salad for our lunch, thinking how empty the cabin feels now that Kay is gone.

The vegetable garden is more of a token of times past. Sooner or later, the deer will come in at night and destroy all the tender young shoots, and Dad will complain. I'll offer solutions that never come to pass. But I can remember a time when Dad harvested enough yellow squash, tomatoes, and okra to fill the back of a farm truck. Mother never cared for gardening much, rebelling whenever Dad walked in carrying a bucket of peas to shell or peaches from his orchard he wanted put up. And who could blame her. She needed a break once in a while. Dad never understood the attitude, but they had different natures. While Dad's is one of busyness, Mom's idea of relaxation was sitting on the sun porch and smoking a few Kent cigarettes.

Late in the evening, Dad complains that his back is bothering him, and I feel like a school teacher who knowingly drove her kids over a cliff. I should have put my foot down about working the garden. I hope he doesn't have another compression fracture. To add insult to injury, he's up and down throughout the night with incontinence, and I find myself mopping up puddles of urine before rummaging through the dresser for clean boxer shorts.

I call Dr. Nolan's office first thing in the morning and make an appointment while Dad stuffs some paperwork into his briefcase for the errands he needs to run in town. I casually mention that maybe we should pick up some Depends in town, but his ego isn't buying it and he changes the subject. He wants to get some different pulls for the dresser, complaining that the old ones are too small to grab. I add the hardware store to my growing list and follow him out the door, running to the house to tell Ben where we're headed.

Getting into the awkward little space of the Ranger pickup is almost Dad's undoing as he eases down into the passenger seat, groaning as he pulls his legs in after him like they're heavy as tree stumps. I shift the gears and let out the clutch as gingerly as possible, but every rut in the gravel drive is a terror. He moans once or twice until I get out to the highway. The professional building is only a few miles away, and I park in a handicap space out front.

We check out the directory inside the door, discovering that Dr. Nolan's office is at the far end of a corridor that looks a mile long. I suggest driving to the other side of the building, but Dad says he'd rather walk, so I lead the way, slow as a pack horse, Dad teetering behind me like a sprung wind-up toy. The nurse wants to know if we brought a urine specimen (we didn't) and Dad says he forgot about it as we take our seats in the waiting room amid other silver-haired octogenarians.

"If I'd known I'd live this long, I'd have taken better care of myself," Daddy whispers with a glib smile. I pat his arm reassuringly, knowing this will be my last full day at the ranch, my last full day of running errands for him. After he disappears into an examination room, I leaf through a magazine with little regard for the pages unfolding before me. I'm still reliving our sleepless night together, trying to erase the scene of Dad sitting on the side of his bed as I hand him a clean pair of boxer shorts. A short time later, Dr. Nolan gives Dad a prescription to treat his kidney infection and we are on our way to the pharmacy and wellness.

To cap off my last afternoon at the cabin, I put the Patsy Cline CD I'd brought into the small boom box on the porch while Dad works on a legal description. He looks up and says I'm spoiling him, but in the next breath says he'd rather listen to something more upbeat, maybe some Lenny Kravitz, something his paramour introduced him to. Oddly enough, that's when she calls. And I don't have to eavesdrop long to figure out the reason for her call. She needs money, and he's more than ready to send it to her. I let my guard down in a most shocking way even to myself, yelling at her from the sidelines, Dad holding the phone away from his ear as we get tangled up in a long-distance cat fight.

After our war of words ends, I feel like a first-class fool, stewing in my director's chair and feeling defeated. My attempt at filing a complaint with Adult Protective Services months earlier failed when the caseworker said there wasn't much he could do because they'd been married. After Dad hangs up, he drops what he's doing and makes an excuse to leave. He says he's forgotten something at the hardware store, but I know he's going to Walmart for a MoneyGram. He never could resist a damsel in distress, and I'm helpless to staunch the flow of cash draining his retirement money. I know there must be a special place in hell reserved for women like her, but I won't embarrass him any further knowing the money isn't going to go for a car repair but up her nose instead.

On a pleasant spring day in the Texas Hill Country, all sins are forgiven. 🪶

Fritzeen, cousin Pam and Kay at pond (Author photo)

Chapter 14 – Fall At The Blue Branch

Texas in the fall isn't much different from Texas in the summer. There's no changing of the guard with respect to color, no leaf peepers booking hotel rooms months in advance. The familiar blast from a shotgun announces the season if you were born a Texan. In October of 2008, after Daddy expressed an interest in attending the Round Top Antique Festival, and with the temperatures backing off somewhat, I booked our flight hoping we could do something fun together. But we've really come to see how he's getting along, and as our plane descends into Austin-Bergstrom it's obvious from the scorched grass that Hurricane Ike didn't track this far west.

The Austin airport is a small, easygoing place with sprawling murals of the Texas landscape above the counters and shops along the curved granite walkways that carry everything Texas, from T-shirts to key chains to brisket at the Salt Lick Café.

131

On our way to the car rental kiosk one level down, I'm pleased to see the addition of a life-sized bronze statue of Barbara Jordan. She's sitting in a large armchair, immersed in a book of law. I remember when she won a seat in the Texas senate, the first black woman to do so. I'd been an admirer of hers for years, and felt she never got her due—at least not from the bigoted male co-workers I associated with decades ago. She was an eloquent speaker, and it saddened me that her failing health kept her from a Supreme Court nomination. That her bronze likeness has been placed in an obscure part of the airport across from the baggage area irks me somewhat, but I guess it's a start.

The air outside is warm and balmy, nothing like the cool fall temps I've grown accustomed to in the Carolinas—the forecast in the low 90's for the coming week. When a young man at the Enterprise kiosk offers us bottled ice water from a cooler, I grab one in surprise and thanks. My throat's been raw and scratchy since we landed, and my eyes sting from the dust in the air.

We load our bags into the trunk of our Chevy Impala, turn the AC on high, and drive out to Texas 71 for the hour-long drive to the ranch. Although it feels good to be home again, Texas feels like another country after so many years away, the landscape a sepia photograph in mellow shades of ochre and brown with a smattering of green where the live oaks and yaupon come into play across the rolling pastures.

"If it weren't for the live oaks the countryside would be dead as a doornail," I say, stating the obvious while phoning Daddy to tell him we'll pick up some brisket sandwiches at Peter's for our lunch.

As we thump across the cattle guard, rounding the sweep under the Perry Oak, I can see Daddy sitting at his work table on the porch of the cabin, no doubt absorbed with a survey. The screen door is missing, the paneled glass door propped open as I run inside, hugging him in a soft embrace, his bones delicate as a baby bird's. He's still wearing a soiled back support that's Velcro'd around his mid-section, none too steady on his feet as he manages to shuffle around the work table and peck me on the cheek. "What happened to the screen door?" I ask. "Oh, it blew off in a bad wind," he smiles, "never got around to replacing it." In the weeks prior to our trip, he said he was fine, but he's just about doubled over as he shuffles back to his chair at the table.

"I bent down to pick up the survey tape last week and felt this sharp pain in my belly. I didn't know what to think, but the doctor says I pulled a muscle and gave me some pills to take. One thing I have to be thankful for is my hands. They're still steady," he says, holding them up for inspection. "I can still work on surveys."

The cabin is about what I expected—a blizzard of newspapers scattered in all directions, file folders stacked in every available chair, six months of dust, grit and house flies on every surface. The fly traps suspended from the ceiling in long yellow curls aren't keeping up. I spot my brother walking across the tracks toward the cabin, a shot gun slung over his shoulder. Dad says he's been dove hunting, and when Ben joins us for lunch, Dan says he wants to eat brisket every day. Ben says he'll grill some doves for supper as we eat our brisket sandwiches. I tell Dad there's a Saudi National bird on his sandwich and he guffaws. He thinks I'm funny.

"God, in his wisdom made the fly," he grins, waving it away, "then forgot to tell us why."

Ben says there should be fresh traps in a kitchen drawer, to microwave one for a few seconds to make it easier to unfurl. After lunch, Dan goes over the floors with the Shop-Vac while I start in on the bathroom, the kitchen sink, and the stovetop. Daddy says he's been having a time figuring out the remote controls for the TV and the satellite dish as we leave to pick up ice, beer, and wine at the HEB, along with a pillow at the Walmart.

Late in the afternoon, the beer iced down, we sit on the porch, passing beers around. I'm not overly surprised when Dad says he's not sure he'll be joining us for the antique festival. He says if he has a place to sit once in a while maybe he can go. When Ben pulls a small camp chair from his truck, Dad nods his approval, but only time will tell. Since Dad takes his laundry to town now, I don't have the added chore of washing sheets and towels. We take over the double bed, moving him to the bunk room, which is closer to the bathroom.

Since catching the red-eye from RDU, we've been up since three a.m., so I'm dog tired. But even with the window unit going, I have trouble sleeping. All the local motels are booked because of the festival or we'd be sleeping at the Best Western. Dad is up and down at least five times during the night, shuffling to the bathroom. Each trip renews my fear that he's going to fall flat on his face given the blackouts he suffered several years ago. Just as the room cools down and I drift off again, Dad gets up, shuffles to the window unit, and turns it off. Despite the two blankets I piled onto his bunk, he chills easily, but I'm too tired to argue.

Dad's the first one up in the morning, driving off in his Suburban before sun-up to get a newspaper in town. After flunking his written driving test the first time, he studied the *Texas Driver's Handbook* and passed. I shudder to think about him out on the road, his license renewed until 2012, the year the Mayan calendar ends.

Over coffee and sticky buns that fill the room with the pleasing scent of cinnamon, Dad says he doesn't think he can get around at the festival without his cane. "I lost it awhile back and haven't replaced it. Y'all go on ahead. I need to work on this plat anyway."

Friday has always been the day to avoid crowds at the festival, although in the aftermath of the recent hurricane, I don't expect the stirred-up anthill of years past. We put on our walking shoes and grab our hats before we set out. Warrenton and Round Top, two bumps in the road, are about fifteen miles away, a pleasant drive through open fields and cow pastures. The traffic is light, and we park in a free lot close to the clutter of tents and out-buildings filled with antiques, junk, and bric-a-brac. One vendor sign reads "Dead People's Stuff" in bold black letters. Our shoes have grown thick with dust in no time at all as I spot some old walking canes here and there, overpriced in most cases.

After lunch at a local café, we're returning to the car when I see some colorful Mexican walking canes dangling from a clothes line. I haven't seen any since my childhood, so I'm afraid to ask the price. I'm mulling over the hand-carved multi-colored sticks when the stocky fellow in the lawn chair says, "Four bucks." Without hesitation, I grab two —one for Dad and one for myself.

Dad seems delighted with the cane, not at all turned off by the bright colors that may help him keep up with it better. We join Ben at the grill behind the house as he checks the doves he's stuffed with jalapeno peppers and wrapped in strips of bacon. Four new plastic lawn chairs have been added to the sitting area under the pecan tree, gifts to Ben from

Dad on Ben's birthday. "These chairs are so cheap I broke one of 'em and had to stack two together," Ben complains.

His comment gets my dander up. After I'd mailed Dad a Walmart gift card for eighty-eight dollars on his eighty-eighth birthday in August, he said he'd spent every penny of it on lawn chairs for Ben, but something isn't adding up right, the thought that his girlfriend enjoyed the rest of it irksome.

Dan and I check into an Austin hotel Sunday afternoon for some much-needed R&R, taking in a band at the Saxon Pub that evening. After stuffing ourselves at the breakfast bar with Texas-shaped waffles and fresh fruit, I drop Dan off at the airport early Monday morning on my way back to the Blue Branch. (I plan to stay on a bit longer). Dad is just finishing his morning beer and says Ben has gone to Galveston to help his stepdaughter repair hurricane damage on her house.

"He'll be away for a few days, and I really need to inspect a lot in Ellinger before I can put a price on the survey."

I offer to drive us there in the Impala, and we eat a buffet lunch at Peter's before heading into town, pulling up to a vacant one-story house sitting on a weedy lot in a rundown neighborhood. I sit in the car with the AC running while Dad grabs his colorful cane, walking along one side of the lot and disappearing behind the house. When he reappears on the other side, it's apparent he's had an accident from the long wet streak running down the front of his khaki slacks. I keep my composure as he eases back into the passenger seat, but I'm cringing inside.

"Well, I had a little accident," he says in somewhat disgusted undertones. "We'll have to head on back so I can change clothes."

"You know, you could cut back on the coffee and beer," I suggest nonchalantly during our drive back to the cabin. "Or you could wear a Depends for your outings."

"Yeah," he says, "but they're so hard to get off over my boots."

I stifle a laugh. I don't understand his logic, but my problem has always been overcoming his objections, so I drop it, wishing he could still enjoy the small pleasures left to him. The small lot surveys that come his way are at least *something* to keep his mind occupied and his ego intact.

After he changes, I toss his soiled clothes into Ben's washing machine before dropping Dad off at Hengst Printing, taking some time for myself to dig a little further into the Perry family tree at the Heritage Center and the court house. While I'm there, I drop by the Jefferson Place, a new assisted living facility I've been meaning to check out. I like the place immediately, the air inside crisp and clean. The living area feels homey, warm, and inviting: muted earth tones on the walls, a big fire place, festive silk arrangements on the tables. A friendly, middle-aged woman invites me into her office, where we discuss Dad's needs along with the pricing for various rooms depending on the size. She hands me a brochure, cautioning me that there's a waiting list. I leave wondering if there's any way in hell I can sell this idea to Daddy. I pick him up at Hengst Printing, parallel parking out front, Dad slipping into the passenger seat ever so gingerly as another car parks behind me. While backing up I wonder aloud how much room I have when Dad says, "When you hear tinkling glass, stop."

Bill collectors have been calling throughout the day as Daddy gives each one the same sob story: "I'm just an old man and I'm having health problems."

Over cheeseburgers and death fries from the Sonic early in the evening, Daddy says Ben won't be back all week. I hate the idea of him living out here by himself. With Jim Kiger gone, there's really nobody around to check on Daddy any more.

"It's just not the same since Jim died," he says, referring to an old friend who passed away after a brief illness.

I nod, knowing there's no way he's going over to keep Jim's widow, Mary, company any time soon, or in the distant future for that matter. She's much too old for him, a mirror reflecting his own advanced age. I leap at this opening and bring up the Jefferson Place, hoping he'll bite.

"I don't think I'm ready for a half-way house just yet," he grins.

In his next breath he expresses his concern about meals, that Ben is running out of meal ideas. No soft foods that he can eat besides hot dogs for lunch. I drive him to the Senior Center just up the road a quarter mile, a place I'd found on the Internet, where he can get a free hot lunch five days a week. He's reluctant to get out of the car, so during our drive back to the cabin I try to emphasize the need to mix with other people more, that the Senior Center would be just the ticket. But I don't think he's buying it. I was hoping to slip over to Wimberley and visit an old friend, but in Ben's absence I stay put. Plus, Daddy has just brought up another issue: He lost his cell phone some time back and doesn't have an instruction manual for his new one. I use the word "new" in loose terms. He says the guy at the Verizon store sold him a used one cheap, on the sly, and it didn't come with a manual.

I'm not sure quite where to start on this venture. Dad seems to think I can just call a store in Austin and they'll mail one out, but this is not the case. After several other phone calls, I get the 800 number for LG customer service, explaining the situation to a friendly voice on the other end. She says they can't send an actual manual, but can mail a photocopy of instructions for Dad's phone. I give her the address.

"I miss Josephine," Daddy sighs, his words a bolt out of the blue.

My heart sinks at the mention of my mother. He's caught me off guard. "I miss her too," I say, thinking back.

I recall the garage sale we had at the family home.

"I feel like I've already died watching my stuff walk out the door," Dad had said.

After the final garage sale at the house on Grouse Moor, Cathy, my friend and former sister-in-law, had suggested the ranch is the best place for him. And maybe he'll be content. Maybe he'll find some modicum of happiness: checking the live trap for the possum raiding his orchard, burning trash, mowing, weekly visits with the county nurse. But his world is shrinking at a frantic pace, almost, but not quite gone, as he loses close friends and future shock catches up with him.

During my last full day at the ranch, Dad asks if I'll help him measure a small out-building at an apartment complex up on the Bluff, so we take my rental car up the winding road that snakes up to Monument Hill State Park, passing the park and locating the apartments—another small job, the smallest I've seen yet, but one that he is determined to tackle. As we pull the tape along each side of the small Laundromat, marking each corner with a pin flag, taking the measurements twice to be sure, he jots down notes on a clip board, seemingly satisfied. Without his work, he is nothing.

I gaze out the window of the 737 as it taxis along the runway and picks up speed, choking back a few tears at lift-off and dabbing my eyes with a tissue as the state of Texas looms far below. I've always been a Daddy's Girl. If Dad thought pierced ears made a woman look cheap, or men with tattoos never amounted to much, I felt the same way until long after I'd left home. I look inward as I sip a glass of wine and gaze at the purity of the cloud formations out my tiny window. If I hadn't moved away, would Dad's situation be any different? I never get any answers.

I picture our last evening together, showing him one more time how to work the remote. I think about our quiet time on the sun porch as his memory drifts into freefall.

"I remember one time when you were just a little girl, we'd come for the weekend. We were heading back to Houston and I said that I wished we could spend every weekend here. And you said, 'But if we came every weekend, it wouldn't' feel special anymore.' And I remember thinking that was such grown-up talk for a girl your age. So insightful."

"Apparently, your quicksilver intellect rubbed off," I said.

"When are you coming back?" he wanted to know. "You're the light of my life," he said as I waved a tearful goodbye from the car.

I'd only been home a few days when Dad called me with some exciting news. It seemed he'd grown bored after I left, so on Labor Day, he decided to take a road trip to Buffalo, a small town outside of Houston, to visit my cousin Gordon, a long tedious drive on back-country roads to get there. He said he enjoyed his visit, that they drank a few beers over lunch before he headed back. During his drive through the township of Ledbetter, a state trooper stopped him. Knowing Dad, there were probably some open beer cans on the floorboard. He said he got stopped for weaving and the trooper took him to the jailhouse.

"The officer was real nice about it. He said I could sit on the couch and watch TV until I could get hold of somebody to come pick me up." I could feel Daddy's grin right through the phone as he spoke. His story had Otis Campbell written all over it.

"So, I called Bonnie, they live over in Anderson, and she and Tony came to my rescue and followed me back to the ranch. So, that's how I spent Labor Day," he chuckled before we hung up.

I fought tooth and claw to get him Meals-On-Wheels. Not an easy task for seniors living in the country. It took weeks of phone calls and lots of begging and cajoling before I managed to hit pay dirt, but the squeaky wheel gets the grease and Dad was very happy with the daily deliveries. And if I live as long as he has, I hope I can hold on to the same spirit and fortitude he's possessed as long as I've been a part of his world. It's really something of a miracle to me how the power of the human spirit can keep pushing onward against a mountain of negative odds.

The author and husband Dan with Sugar at the corn crib, 1993

Chapter 15 – The Best Little B&B In Texas

Joy is a component of life, or should be.
— LADY BIRD JOHNSON

May of 2009: I'm late getting here this year. The bluebonnet season has come and gone because my friends, Kay, Fritzeen, and yours truly couldn't get our acts together in time. I was determined that we'd give Dad his space and spend our evenings in the luxury of a nice motel, but all area motels were booked solid through April due to all those people coming to see the wildflowers.

When Fritzeen dropped out because her elderly mother had an infection, I decided to book a room for myself and Kay at a local B&B in La Grange. It's on the pricey side, but not too bad if we split the cost. And I think we both deserve a little pampering for a change. In some ways I'm glad to be here in May for a change of pace. Just outside the Austin airport, driving along Highway 71, I'm seeing wildflowers I'd almost forgotten about—the ones that take over after all the bluebonnets have gone to seed.

I phone Dad to tell him I'm on my way, taking in the patches of black-eyed Susans blooming along the roadside, acres of Indian blanket and yellow coreopsis lighting up the fields like gold. I pass a field of prickly white poppies that look like new-fallen snow, thinking what a breathtaking picture it would make. But I hate to keep Daddy waiting and decide to press on, rolling up and down the hills through Bastrop and Smithville.

I drive through a brief shower before approaching the ranch gate an hour later. The pasture is a profusion of Mexican hats swaying in the breeze as I tap the brakes of my Chevy Cobalt, rolling slowly over the cattle guard to take in the view. The pump jack is sitting idle when I pull around the Perry Oak and park at the back of the cabin. Dad is hunched over his worktable and I lean across it to peck him on the cheek, resting my hand on his bony shoulder. His shirt looks like it's draped over a coat hanger as he half- stands in a crippled fashion, bracing against the edge of the table for support.

"Well, I see you made it. So glad you're here," he grins.

"Great Caesar's ghost, Daddy, where's the work table? Are you sure it's under there somewhere?"

I'm usually on a high when I arrive, but it soon passes when I see the state of the cabin and Dad's declining health. He's still wearing his back brace even though he says his back is doing fine. He always paints a rosy picture over the phone, but the truth always wins out sooner or later.

"We just haven't had any survey work in months. And I'm having a heck of a time keeping up with my bills and all my mail. Maybe you can help me while you're here."

The air is humid and sticky against my skin, but not overly hot. Flies are darting about the porch like a mutant army and I turn on the ceiling fan, hoping to ward them off. There's a nice breeze coming through the jalousies and I'm trying to ignore the flies when my brother appears in the doorway. We make small talk and right away I notice the Mexican cane I bought my last trip is missing.

"I don't know what happened to it," Dad begins.

Ben picks up the conversation: "He could have left it anywhere, Sue. It could be in town somewhere, or it may even be in the back of his Suburban."

I'm disappointed about the cane. As I offer to pick up some brisket in Ellinger for our lunch, little scenarios on its whereabouts keep flashing through my head. Dad says he'll come along for the ride and grabs his new black metal cane, one I'm already developing a hatred for. He always wants to see what kind of car I'm driving and get the feel of it even if it's a compact car he needs a shoehorn to squeeze into.

During the drive, Dad says he checked out the Jefferson Place Retirement Community and really likes it. But he's not sure he can swing living there and keep up with the ongoing expenses at the ranch. In other words, he's built his house of straw. I shudder to think where the money will come from if he suffers a debilitating stroke. I'm sure he's still sending money to the Houston hussy, and he must have read my mind. He got the Scotch-Irish gene from Granddad's side of the family: short arms and deep pockets. Careful with his money to the point of being a tightwad, he says he only sends her fifty dollars a month, but I'm not buying it.

In the twelve years since Mom died, I've discovered he's just a man—a red-blooded man with male appetites—and I keep seeing a side of him I've never seen before. Or maybe I didn't want to see. You read from time to time about men living a double life, and I sometimes wonder if philandering was the real cause of my mother's mental problems. I have to fight back pangs of jealousy and resentment, but when he looks across the table at me with a broad smile, my reserve melts like a chocolate bar left out in the sun. He's a charmer and a disaster, and he seems to be disintegrating before my very eyes.

Later on, we somehow manage to clear the survey files and folders he's stacked in each of the three extra chairs we'll need for my cousins, Pam and Lauran, and possibly a friend, who are expected for a visit on Saturday, though the table seems like a hopeless cause.

"I still keep a log book," Dad says, flipping over to a fresh page. "But the phone isn't ringing at all unless it's a bill collector. I write down various events of my day anyhow. Let's see, Susan arrived at noon." He jots this down with a No. 3 pencil.

I've not yet told him that Kay and I won't be sleeping in the cabin this trip. He won't like it, but he'll adapt. Maybe it was intuition, or maybe I just remembered the sleepless nights of my last trip, that awful, bone-chilling night terror he had, screaming bloody murder and scaring me half to death. But I'm determined not to get stressed out about the state of things in Dad's life. At least I hope I can pull it off. Aside from that, I'm no spring chicken anymore. Cleaning the cabin wears me out. I keep telling myself that I'm not going to clean the jalousies and the plate glass windows with Glass Plus. I'm not going to scour out the metal sink in the kitchenette or the shower stall, or vacuum the floors, though I'm not opposed to tidying up and straightening a bit here and there at my leisure.

The usual boiled cabbage odor on the porch is faint, but the cabin itself has a stale old-man smell about it, and as the afternoon wears on, I break down and strip his bed. I know he takes his laundry to the Suds 'N Duds now, but his bed is a shambles. He puts up a small fuss when I decide it's time to dispose of his moth-eaten pillows.

"I'm going to burn these two pillows," I say flatly, waiting for the fallout.

"What's wrong with those pillows?" he wants to know.

"Just look at them. They're hideous. They're covered in stains, just a breeding ground for dust mites."

I pick up a pair of cheap pillows at the Dollar General, two for six bucks, and, upon my return, I finally get around to telling Dad that I'll be sleeping at the old Killough House over the weekend. The B&B is called Brendan Manor now, but we'll always think of that big, pale-pink stucco manse with its rust-colored awnings as the Killough House since my grandparents were close friends of John and Nellie Killough back in the day. In a way, it might be fun for Dad to see the inside of the house again after so many years. I tell him I need to check in around three o'clock, and he seems happy to drive into town with me. I've never been inside the house, so I'm anxious to see if the pictures I pulled up on the web are in keeping with the actual décor, if it's truly the "Best Little B&B in Texas."

The grand dame of La Grange sits on an acre of manicured lawn and sprawling live oaks on the main drag into town. As we pull through the entry gates and into the portico to park, Dad says he hasn't been here since the age of ten. I help him up the steep steps to a wicker chair on the concrete side porch where a note with my name on it is tacked to the door. The innkeepers are away for the evening, but they've left me the combination to the entry door along with their cell phone numbers in case I have any problems.

"Cool. We may have the whole place to ourselves," I say.

I press the numbers into a well-worn brass dial on one of the double doors and it swings open with a loud creaking noise. The air inside is chilly and wonderful. I motion for Dad and he grabs his cane and follows me inside. "It's cold enough to hang hogs in here," he complains. "It feels good." We stand in the foyer, admiring the ornate staircase and the afternoon light coming through the panel of stained glass on the landing as I recognize the music from "Phantom of the Opera" playing in the background. All through the years, whenever we made trips to La Grange, I'd pass this house in awe, imagining the finery contained inside its walls. The ceilings look twenty feet tall, but Dad says they're eight feet as we make our way from room to room, his cane making a clink, clink sound each time it hits the floor behind me.

We head across the spacious living room, divided into two sitting areas of overstuffed sofas, antique chairs and oriental rugs, before peering into the dining room where two glass cabinets full of Royal Doulton prop up the wallpapered walls. Lace curtains in the ceiling-to-floor windows let in filtered light as we wind our way back around to the study, where a large oil painting of Mr. Killough himself, cigar in hand, hangs above the slate fireplace.

Dad is having the time of his life, a big grin on his face, God love him. Before we leave, I dig my camera out of my roll-on, snapping a few pictures of him standing at the staircase before running up the stairs to see my room, passing a glass chest full of Hummel figurines on the landing.

The Nellie Lee Room, named after one of the Killough daughters, was once the master suite, the windows of the large corner room looking out to the front lawn. It's everything I'd expected and more—roomy enough to hold a square dance in. No detail has been overlooked in the decorating of the two oversized twin sleigh beds that are heaped with decorative pillows and throws. Wingback chairs sit to the side of each bed, along with two writing desks positioned at opposite sides of the room. A massive mirrored wardrobe ties the room together; I have no complaints when I spot a small cable TV nestled in the far corner and a claw-foot tub in the cramped bathroom.

On our drive back to the Blue Branch, I daydream aloud, wondering what the innkeepers had to pay for such a place.

"You could probably find out at the Appraisal District," Dad says.

"Must have cost a small fortune. Not to mention all the antique furniture and those Thomas Kincaid's on the walls." I say.

"Thomas Kincaid? Who the heck is that?" Dad says.

Kay is outside visiting with Ben when we return late in the afternoon. We crack open a couple of Coronas on the porch and her eyes light up when I give her a report on the B&B. A hummingbird appears, hovering outside the window before darting, then pausing as it makes its way around the porch searching for sugar water.

"We should pick up a hummingbird feeder when we're in town," Kay suggests with her usual enthusiasm.

"Last time I bought a bird feeder, it ended up full of wasp nests instead of sugar water," I lament, remembering how I tried to dig them out with a coat hanger before tossing the whole thing into the trash.

With nothing on the agenda for supper, we decide to eat at the Guadalajara Mexican Café in town, so I head over to the big house to tell Ben. He's just getting over a bout of bronchitis and says he'll take a rain check. On our way out, I spot a scissor-tailed flycatcher perched on the barbed wire fence. Aside from the roadrunner, it's my favorite Texas bird, and I creep along the gravel as the flycatcher swoops to the ground for a bug, then lights back on the wire, showing its salmon-pink underbelly.

We have our pick of tables at the Guadalajara, unusual for a Friday night. I guess the slack economy has caught up with one of my favorite budget eateries as well. Dad complains that he's having trouble keeping his pants up and yanks on his belt as the waitress seats us at a booth at the window.

"You need some suspenders," Kay suggests over a frozen Margarita. "Maybe we can stop somewhere on the way back. It's still early. Beal's should be open."

Dad orders chicken quesadillas and eats one before deciding he doesn't care for them. "I always seem to order the wrong thing," he complains as the waiter gives us a take-out carton.

After supper we wait in the car while Kay runs into Beal's, a small department store on the way home. She comes back out shaking her head. No luck.

"Before you leave, I need you to show me how to work the remote again," Dad says. "Kerry wrote down some instructions when he was here, and Ben shows me, but then I can't get the TV to work and he gets disgusted with me."

We decode the remote control for Dad, going over the buttons a few times, but I don't think it's sinking in. Although I have trouble with electronics myself, I can't dismiss the early stages of dementia. Coming from an engineer who once positioned offshore rigs using the Pole star, Dad's diminishing ability to manage little technical tasks disturbs me. Nowadays, the GPS has taken the place of his intricate calculations, but I can remember the evening he hadn't shown up for supper, asking Mom where he was—it was not unusual for him to be "out in the field."

"He's shooting Polaris," she said, further explaining it to me.

I don't understand it now, and I didn't back then. I never got that math gene. Calculus, logarithms, and slide rules were never part of my makeup. Dad takes his usual position in the oak rocking chair. Weathered to a dark patina, the chair was bought by my grandparents when he was a newborn. We visit on the porch for a while until he starts yawning.

I grope for the pocket light I always carry to make out the numbers on the combination lock on the door of the B&B just as another couple pulls up the drive in a Porsche Cayman.

"Leave it to Susan to have a flashlight," Kay laughs as she walks inside. "Oh, my God! It's magnificent!"

"Decadent, but in such good taste," I concur.

The couple the Porsche belongs to soon join us in the butler's pantry for homemade brownies and some chewy, delectable cookies left under a glass dome on the granite bar. We introduce ourselves and visit as I open the cheap bottle of merlot I picked up at the HEB. Michael says he and his wife have stayed here before. He has just flown in from Utah to look for a piece of ranch property in the area, lamenting that property around Austin and the Hill Country has gone out of sight.

Later, I'm wishing for an elevator as I lug my two suitcases up the stairs, listening to Kay as she raves about everything.

"I haven't stayed in very many B&B's. None as nice as this one, that's for sure," she smiles as we settle into our room. "Oh look, chocolate mints! And terry cloth bath robes!"

I feel like I'm flying in first class while poor Daddy's stuck back in coach. I invited him over for breakfast in the morning, but he said nine o'clock is too late for him, that he eats around six.

A fresh fruit salad served in champagne glasses drenched in a delectable vanilla yogurt sauce is our first course at breakfast, followed by Scotch eggs baked in small tureens and hidden under layers of cheese and ham. It was all I could do to pry Kay out of bed around eight-thirty. I think she would have slept all day if I'd let her, but she's bright and bubbly at the dining room table, and everyone is taken with her. Nobody at the table has any inkling of her past, making the local paper as she sent cold-blooded murderers and rapists to the slammer. As she trills on like a nightingale, it's hard to believe she lost her brother this past Christmas, along with her brother-in-law who died suddenly of a stroke. Her sister is now selling the *Cloud 9*, the sailboat they'd lived in during retirement, the boat Kay had spent so many happy times on. Maybe Brendan Manor is just what the doctor ordered. Kay has always been a people person, unlike yours truly, the would-be novelist, who hangs out in front of a computer every day, living in an imaginary world with imaginary people, hoping to crank out something worthy of publication.

The innkeepers join us at the table for light conversation, eager to answer any questions we might have about Brendan Manor as we learn that the Victorian staircase was imported from New Orleans, the house built around it in the early 1800s.

"The windows are hand-blown French Quinn," the husband continues, "and the red-glass panel above the front door is called 'pigeon-blood red.'"

He's a pleasant man of some bearing, with silver-gray hair, but when he says he's a retired Baptist preacher from Conroe I start to feel like a cornered rat. What I *really* want to know is how much this manse set them back, but I don't have the nerve to ask. At ten-thirty, the conversation around the table showing no signs of ending, I make a motion to leave.

"Well, I guess I need to get on back to Grey Gardens."

Kay jumps up, but not before Michael encourages us to join them around eight o'clock for some live music at The Bugle Boy, a local listening room in a converted Army barrack that I've always meant to visit but never got around to. My cell phone rings on our way out. It's my cousin Pam. She and Lauran are about a half hour away. Where should we meet? I tell her we're on our way to the cabin.

Dad meets us on the porch, having just returned from the Walmart with a pair of red suspenders. He's removed his Velcro back brace, and after we help him adjust the straps and get the silver clamps clipped to his slacks, we stand back and admire how nice they look with his red checkered shirt. Ben is out on the tractor mowing the lower pasture when we decide to take our usual hike around the loop, hoping he hasn't mowed down all the wildflowers. The Mexican hats are thick as thieves, but during our walk, we notice small clusters of horse mint growing along the foot path. Further back, growing along the tree line, are the white umbrella-like flowers of Queen Anne's lace, and as we hike to the far side, just past the second deer blind, Kay snaps my picture in a stand of yellow tickseed. I've already sweated through my cotton blouse, and just as we cross over the railroad track, I see Pam and Lauran walking our way. You can tell we're cousins from our dark hair and brown eyes, though we all cheat these days with bottles of Clairol. Their father was Dad's younger brother Lelldon, killed in a car wreck in Baghdad, Iraq, when we were kids. Alethea, a Houston friend I haven't seen in many years, is lagging behind them and smiling broadly.

All this female attention is doing wonders for Daddy's morale, though I miss the sweet tea and spicy talk of the past. When Lauran presents him with a new cotton shirt in a navy plaid along with a cheesecake from the Cheesecake Factory, Daddy comes to life like a hothouse flower, laughing and cutting up like he used to. Pam starts handing out neck coolers, strips of cloth containing pockets of crystals that hold water.

We all begin to laugh as we loop them around our necks and realize that the navy one Alethea grabbed matches her blouse; the tan one matches my yellow blouse of white orchids on tan stems. I'm feeling so light-headed that I might just float away. As Daddy snaps open a can of Miller Lite, Pam says she's starving. Neither Kay nor I have an appetite after such a bountiful breakfast, so I encourage them to go on into town and try the Bistro on the square. I fix a tuna sandwich for Dad, saying we'll meet up with them later for a nature hike on Monument Hill.

By the time we reach the Bluff that overlooks the Colorado River the temperature has dropped ten degrees. As we look out over the murky green waters of the Colorado far below, dark ominous clouds are building to the north, the wind whipping at our clothes. The cool front is moving in faster than we'd expected, and after a spritz of rain is followed by a clap of thunder, we ditch our plans for a nature hike, winding our way back down the Bluff. Alethea wants to know where she can get a cup of coffee, so we swing by Brendan Manor, killing two birds with one stone. She and the cousins had hoped to book a room for Saturday night and want to see the place I'd suggested. "It's fabulous!" I hear Pam exclaim as Kay gives them the grand tour and I brew a cup of Joe for Alethea using the new-fangled coffee-maker on the mirrored bar of the study. By the time we reach the cabin again, rain is pelting the tin roof. Dad says the suspenders aren't working out. They won't fit around his back brace and he's glad they didn't cost much. Lauran serves up the cheesecake and talks about her new venture working from home before they head out. I hate to see them go. Pam and I are a year apart and have always been close. She's been helpful looking into senior care for Dad, always finding information and services I've overlooked.

Dancing to music from the Weather Channel, Kay grabs the hand weights I gave Dad last Father's Day and goes through some of her exercise routines in the cramped space on the porch.

"I don't know why Lauran brought me that shirt," Dad says. "I don't need any shirts. My clothes rack in the bunk room is full of shirts."

I'm thinking old and threadbare, but don't say it out loud. I'm still not hungry at suppertime, so we heat up the leftover quesadillas in the microwave for Dad. This time around he seems to be enjoying them, sharing what's left with Kay before we head over to The Bugle Boy.

I'm up with the chickens Sunday morning, leaving Kay looking like a corpse in her bed while I tip-toe down the stairs in my deluxe bath robe, brewing a cup of hazelnut decaf before I sit out on the side porch and sneak a cigarette. Two wrens, unhappy about my presence, keep scolding me as they try to feed their babies nesting in a basket of begonias nearby.

The morning is chilly and overcast. After a breakfast of French toast and eggs scrambled in cream cheese, crystal vases of red Knock Out roses on the table, I phone Dad to come join us for coffee.

"I've been so constipated. I just finished taking an enema," he says, "but I'll be over shortly."

I'm relieved when the other guests head out for church and we have the house to ourselves. We linger in the living room where Kay is wrapped up in a blanket on the sofa and says she'll head back to Houston after she wakes up. I hope Dad isn't going to mention the enema, pulling back the drapes and pointing out the wrens at the flower basket as his Suburban appears through the window; minutes later, he's asking for coffee. "This coffee's gotten cold. Can you heat it up?" Dad asks. I microwave the coffee and bring him a plate of cookies. "Now it's too hot. Can you bring me some ice?" I don't know where I'll stay for the next three nights, though the innkeeper offered me our room at a reduced rate if I stay. The Best Western is more reasonably priced, so I decline his offer, knowing how empty the Nellie Lee room will feel without Kay. It's hard to say goodbye to her thinking it may be another blasted year before we're back together again. Though we keep up through emails pretty regularly, it's just not the same. As the sky starts clearing, we snap a few pictures on the front lawn as she points out the yellow blooms of a jacaranda bush in the landscape. I break down when we hug. She's been such a true friend and uplifting presence in my life. And I know Dad will miss her as well.

As soon as I see the barn doors open each morning, visible through the bathroom window, I join Ben there to visit and plan the evening meal. It's a beautiful day with highs in the seventies and a stiff breeze. I've been nursing chigger bites for days, careful not to sit on the door jamb like I'd been doing, listening while he voices his concerns about the lack of survey work. He's just finished restoring a set of dining room chairs that were damaged in Hurricane Ike, hoping to deliver them to his stepdaughter Lexi, come Memorial Day weekend, looking forward to taking his two grandchildren to the beach in Galveston.

"The doctor said these painkillers I take for my back would make me constipated, but I sure wish I could get back to being regular again," Dad complains, shuffling to his plastic patio chair at the worktable.

I'm wondering if this is something he writes in his log book as I make a quick trip to the Walmart, stopping to admire the baskets of petunias in red, pink, and deep purple on display out front. I indulge myself with a small pot of Texas lantana, smiling at its cheerful orange and yellow blooms and trying to remember the last time I planted anything at the Blue Branch. Mom's grave could use some fresh flowers as well, but there's nothing that thrills me in the silk bins. Armed with stool softeners and laxatives, I head for the check-out.

In the early afternoon, we decide to drive over to Fayetteville to look around and see if any shops are open. It's a close escape with a scenic drive on one of the back roads. I slow down to admire some longhorn cattle grazing in a pasture outside of town while Dad sips his Miller Lite. As we circle the town square, Dad points to one of the shops. "Mom's Cleopatra beauty shop was over there," he says. Nothing looks open as we circle the near-deserted square a second time and on the drive back Dad says he needs to pee. I pull onto a discreet feeder road that's hidden behind an embankment and park with the motor running.

"I feel dizzy," he says through the open window. "I need to stretch out."

I dash around the car, opening the back door and grabbing his arm. As I back the car out to the highway, he says he's feeling okay, but I'm riding on pins and needles all the way back. Once we're safely inside the cabin, I read the label on the bottle of hydrocodone he takes for back pain, pointing out the bright red tag: *No alcohol. May cause dizziness.*

On Monday morning, Daddy meets me at the breakfast bar of the Best Western and I make him a waffle.

"I'd rather have a doughnut if they have any," he says, and I explain that they only have muffins. "I don't know why you'd spend good money on a motel when you could stay in the cabin for free," he says. He's wearing a tattered long-sleeved shirt, a faded red, to fight off the morning chill. "Why didn't you wear that nice blue shirt Lauran gave you?"

"I think it's ugly."

Back at the cabin, he's intent on updating his life insurance, so we spend a few tedious hours going through file folders of old outdated policies dating back to 1957, making some phone calls about beneficiaries. He seems a little incoherent at times, and it scares me to think his mind is slipping. I take into account the hydrocodone, advising him to stop taking it for a while and see what happens, or to cut out the six beers he drinks every day. Six that I *know* about. I take a much-needed break to plant the lantana. I'm going to put it right outside the cabin door where it gets morning sun and afternoon shade. If it thrives, it'll add a nice splash of color for years to come. I dig the hole, wishing for my garden gloves, but it feels good to get some Blue Branch dirt under my fingernails again.

After a lunch of ham sandwiches, I'm ready to ditch the insurance policies for a while and work on something else, something we might be able to finish easily, sorting through dusty old surveys that belong in storage. While he sorts, I start tossing them into the trailer behind the riding mower for the short trip to his workshop. Inside the workshop, I tell Dad that we should load the bottom drawers first so the cabinet won't tip over, discovering a stash of skin flicks in the process, recoiling like I'd just uncovered a box of rattlesnakes. I slam the drawer on *College Girls Gone Wild* as Dad says very casually that's his sex drawer. With that, I walk on back to the cabin in disgust. *Too much information!*

Dad phones my room early Tuesday morning. He can't make the breakfast bar. Now he's so regular he's afraid to stray too far from the bathroom. I bring him another apple from the fruit bowl mid-morning, and he says he needs a ride to Hengst Printing to drop off some typing. I could find Hengst Printing blindfolded, but every time we come, Dad points out the street to turn on. This time I raise my voice, snapping that I know the way.

"Well, you don't have to bite my head off," he says, looking hurt.

I feel like crawling under the seat, hating myself for lashing out. I do see how being a caregiver on a daily basis takes a special kind of person, and it makes me wonder if I could handle Dad's care full time like my friend Fritzeen's been doing for the last ten years. If I lived close by, I could drop in for a few hours here and there and help him instead of pulling my hair out trying to work under a deadline.

I apologize, clearing the air, helping Daddy with his small, light-weight briefcase after parking out front. Hengst Printing caters to the local high school and the store is chocked full of T-shirts and sweat shirts and printing supplies. I never tire of looking over all manner of paraphernalia that you can slap an emblem on, from mugs to key chains.

In late afternoon, I join my brother for beer and conversation under the pecan tree behind the big house. He's grilling ribs on one of the barbecue pits he made when we all lived in Houston so many years ago. The legs have long since sunk into the ground and the wheels are submerged in weeds. Since Dad handed his tongs over to Ben, he's become the resident Grillmeister, adding pecan chips to the fire box and taking great pride in his culinary skills. We talk about Dad some, but only if I bring it up. Dad will be here all alone on Memorial Day weekend, and while I don't begrudge Ben the need to get away, I do worry. What if he falls? "He always has his cell phone in his pocket, Sue." I don't mention the other what ifs: What if he's knocked unconscious? What if he suffers a stroke? "Dad told me about that assisted living place in town, but I don't see how he can swing it. He'll still want to spend every day here, Susan."

I guess he's right. Daddy will live or die on his own terms. On my last day, Dad says that Kerry is planning a trip from Colorado come August. He wants to know if I can come, too. I have to hold back my tears thinking about it. It's been a long time since we've all been together. On the other hand, the cabin is a nice place to be in the cooler weather, but not in the summertime when the sun beats through the tin roof like a hammer. I leave it open as to whether I'll make it.

Dad needs to pay some bills but he can't find any stamps. I make a brief shakedown of the worktable and in a last-ditch effort, I open the old leather briefcase he keeps at the foot of his bed. Imagine my shock when I discover an empty bottle of Viagra. *Good Lord*!

During my drive to the Austin airport, a white pickup passes me on the left a few miles outside of La Grange, just a typical pickup truck with a wooden gun rack in the rear window. Only instead of a deer rifle nesting in the rack, I spot a Mexican cane. *Jiminy Cricket*! What are the odds? But I don't have the wherewithal to give chase and get into an argument with a complete stranger. It's one of those little happenings I'll chalk up to coincidence, though I couldn't shake the image the rest of that day.

On Memorial Day weekend, the distress call comes in. Daddy says he's stony broke until the first of the month when his pension and social security checks come in. Could I send him some money? I'm shocked, and at the same time resigned, listening as he explains how he's gotten behind on the auto insurance and now Allstate is threatening to cancel.

My blood curdles when he goes on about taking out a loan at one of those loan-shark places in Giddings, thankful when he says they won't give him another loan due to his bad credit rating.

I'm reliving Father's Day 2007 all over again, right before he lost the Houston house; it's hard to say no, but I'm wondering where all the cash is really going. I'm sure this was all brewing before I ever left the state, and my greatest fear is that he'll get in so deep he'll end up jeopardizing the ranch. I'm trying to erase the image of that nice couple we met at the Brendan Manor—the couple in the market for ranch property.

He gives me the phone number of his insurance agent, and I tell him I'll handle it. guess I'm going to be his social secretary from a thousand miles away. In the meantime, he's almost out of gas and beer and I promise I'll run to the Walmart and send a Money-Gram to get him through the weekend. Will a hundred dollars be enough? It's hard to put a price on loneliness.

Left to right: the author, Ivan, and cousins Lauran and Pam

Chapter 16 – Something You Can't See

...and if there is
A fly nearby, or dust, a blowing curtain,
The sun coming in through the glass, watch it:
That is yours to keep.

— FIDDLEDEEDEE, BY SHELBY STEPHENSON

I hadn't been back to Texas in the wintertime in six years, not since the time Daddy blacked out, fell into the creek, and broke his wrist. That particular January had been pleasant, balmy, every day bright with glorious sun. But the weather in central Texas can be fickle, and like Texas weather, Daddy's health had taken another turn.

I landed at Austin-Bergstrom to a wet gray blanket of a day, the icy wind harsh against my face as I raced from the terminal to pick up my rental car, dreading the chill I'd find in the cabin, phoning my brother when I reached Bastrop, a town halfway to the ranch. The countryside along Texas 71 was as bleak as the weather, the fields to either side of the highway a sea of frost-bitten grass, a stand of pines around Bastrop adding a bit of contrast to the gray landscape. The pump jack in the front pasture stood idle as I thumped over the cattle-guard and slowly made my way along the rutted gravel road, creeping under the Perry Oak, ragged puffs of smoke billowing from the chimney a welcome sight. I parked at the cabin, and once inside, I found a small radiant heater glowing red, the oven door propped open. Even so, the room felt cold as a meat locker. Ben was nowhere to be found as I unloaded my bags, but he soon appeared on the sun porch and said he'd been gathering firewood, his breath turning to fog as he spoke. Dressed in a camouflage coverall, a navy stocking cap pulled over his ears, he said deer season ended on Sunday and, as I popped the trunk of the silver-gray Ford Focus using the remote key, he added that he hoped to bag another buck.

"The salesman said it takes a while to heat up, but it should keep the room warm enough," I said, referring to the radiant heater I'd picked up in Bastrop as he carried the heavy box to the porch, tore into it and removed the packing material. "After I get it plugged in, I'm going to the nursing home to see Daddy."

"He's more alert in the mornings," Ben said. "That's when I usually visit. It can be depressing at times. One morning I saw a woman picking out the lining for her coffin."

We didn't discuss supper, although the taco I'd eaten in a rush at the airport was long gone. I was thankful I'd packed all of my long underwear along with some fleece. The electric blanket worked, just barely, and I'd need it to keep from freezing to death overnight. Ben offered me the back bedroom of the big house, but he goes to bed early, not to mention getting to the bathroom in the middle of the night is an obstacle course from one end of the house to the other, so I opted out. I turned off the oven before I left, uncomfortable with the idea of using it as a heater and disgusted by the rancid smell it gave off.

I drove into town through a fine gray mist, warm at last inside the rental car, passing City Cemetery where my mother is buried, thinking about the need for some fresh flowers for her grave, thinking about a verse from Ecclesiastes—"One generation passeth away and another generation cometh, but the earth abideth forever"—when I took a wrong turn at the town square. I realized my mistake and headed north over the railroad tracks, pulling into the parking lot of the nursing home, crestfallen at the sight of the low-slung brick building that dated back to the 1950s. A number of shrunken, white-haired residents slumped in wheelchairs greeted me with twisted smiles as I passed through the living area where a large-screen TV blared from a far wall. The room was pleasant enough, with a modicum of furniture, knickknacks, and silk arrangements set around to make it look homey. So, this is how it ends. So, this is the end of the line. "The beginning of the end," as one friend put it. I could have wrung her neck when she said it. Even false hope is better than no hope.

I stopped at the nursing station, a circular affair with hallways that fanned out like the spokes of a wagon wheel. I asked directions to Mr. Perry's room, and a pleasant, middle-aged woman looked up from her computer screen and smiled, pointing down the first hallway toward room 612. I made my way down the polished linoleum floors of the long corridor, passing rooms where other patients were either engrossed in their television programs or visiting with family.

A big orange sign on Daddy's door said I'd have to gown up before entering. I hesitated at the door, not knowing what to expect. He'd been suffering from C diff., or colitis, brought on from the powerful antibiotics he'd been given for his post-surgical pneumonia, another setback to his recovery from a broken hip. I found him fast asleep, his white hair splayed out on the pillow like a patch of unruly weeds, his mouth hanging open as the TV at the foot of his bed resonated with some dull country music. Daddy never cared much for television. He'd rather be outside getting things done: working his garden, mowing, clearing brush, puttering in his workshop or plotting a survey. He'd lost the ability to swallow after the surgery, a brownish fluid that reminded me of a milkshake flowing through a tube to his stomach peg, his lifeline for over a month.

"He'll make a full recovery," the surgeon had said.

I could have cried at the sight of him. Never before had I felt so powerless, so frightened of the nearness of death. I set my purse on a chair and leaned over his gaunt face, so hollowed out since his hip replacement. He looked as though he'd just come from the death mills at Auschwitz; it was hard to remember the man who used to jog two miles every morning before heading to the office; it was hard to watch a man once so energetic and alive with busyness lying prone in a hospital bed. He'd never been sick a day in his life. By the same token, he'd not been well for a long time—not since osteoporosis started hampering his mobility, attacking his bones like a swarm of hungry termites. He suffered his first hip fracture riding a four-wheeler across a bumpy pasture at the age of eighty-five. I never thought of him as elderly until compression fractures followed one by one, and a series of back surgeries left him doubled over like Quasimodo.

Blackouts came in rapid succession until he got his pacemaker, but despite all of these setbacks, Dad never lost his drive to keep going, drawing up meets and bounds in his makeshift office on the sun porch, mowing the grassy areas between the house and the pasture, setting varmint traps in his fruit orchard, or stocking the pond with channel cats. Then he took a spill in the cabin and his right hip shattered like glass. When the doctor told him that he'd need a hip replacement, that his hip was too deteriorated, Daddy said he'd like to go home and think it over.

"Keep me going," he'd whispered to my brother through an oxygen mask in the ICU.

He stirred as I gently rubbed his arm but didn't come fully awake, and I gazed at the small black-and-white photograph I'd carried to the hospital at Christmas, the one of Daddy, Ben, and me riding donkeys at the Ace-Ranch-Motel in Kerrville when we were small. By the time we graduated to horses, Daddy had made friends with Mr. Stout, the owner. One day, after we'd picked out our horses, Mr. Stout walked out of the stable with a high-spirited chestnut roan many hands high, handing the reins to Dad. I had my doubts about Dad's ability as a horseman, but he said he'd give it a try. The minute Dad put one foot in the stirrup, the horse bucked and churned and he'd barely swung into the saddle when the horse took off like it was running the Preakness, slinging caliche every which way. Dad jerked on the reins and came to a flying stop, bouncing back in our direction with a big grin on his face. He made a few more laps up and down the road-turned-racetrack before he dismounted. Whether this was Mr. Stout's idea of a joke I'll never know, but Dad took it in stride. Said the horse packed too much punch for his taste. Frightened as I was that day, he made it look easy. And I'll always carry that image of him, laughing in spite of the danger. Happy trails. Happy memories.

I lingered at his bedside for a while, suddenly feeling exhausted from the trip, thinking about an email I'd received from my cousin Pam the previous week that cautioned: "Don't forget to take care of yourself."

It was way past suppertime and I needed to eat, past the time Ben would have eaten and settled down with a Bud Light in front of his television. In his prime he was a dead ringer for Richard Boone from *Have Gun Will Travel.* I still see the similarities, though I have to imagine the character Paladin with gray hair, and reading glasses. He never signed on as Daddy's caregiver, and he's feeling overwhelmed with the responsibilities—another reason for my trip.

I wolfed down a cheeseburger at the Sonic before heading to the ranch. When I reached the cabin, the room felt about the way I'd left it, cold enough to hang hogs. The light over the sink had burned out, but in the dim light from a table lamp I could read the thermometer at the window: sixty degrees inside, dipping below forty outside. I went to the bathroom closet to get a new bulb only to discover the overhead light there was out as well. It was too high for Daddy to reach, possibly something my brother wouldn't think to check, possibly something Daddy felt too proud to ask assistance with.

I decided to forgo a shower my first night and poured myself a glass of wine. I could have drowned in a river of it. As I unpacked, I brought up the Weather Channel and hung up some of Daddy's shirts, most of them long-sleeved, most of them frayed at collar and cuff. What a disastrous twist of fate, I thought to myself. Going from a comfortable home in Houston and moving to the cabin after his money ran out, his modest pension and Social Security the only cushion he has left to fall back on.

"You're not being fair to your children," the lawyer had scolded as we sat together in her La Grange office and she explained the foreclosure notice on his Grouse Moor house and the pending lawsuits from debt collectors.

The cabin was never meant to be anything more than a weekend retreat. And since it has no closets, the clutter factor has posed a problem since Daddy moved in. Prior to my last visit, Ben had defrosted the mini-fridge and cleared off the drop-leaf table, the shelves of canned goods somewhat depleted. I tidied up even further, laundering the essence of old man from the bed sheets and scouring the sink of the kitchenette. "Prudence Pots the Pan Inspector," Daddy used to call me. And for good reason: I've been this way since girlhood. I remember asking him what they used to scour pots and pans in the olden days. When he said they used old coffee grounds or sand, I could scarcely believe it. I could have used a hazmat team on the bathroom, but eventually I got it into shape for Daddy's homecoming. But it's been six weeks since his hip surgery and he's hanging by a thread and looking for a rope.

As the Weather Channel went into radar mode, with wispy rain clouds sweeping across the nation, the guitar riffs from an old Pink Floyd album, "Wish You Were Here," rang out like a death knell. It fit my somber mood. I'd never been alone in the cabin before, never spent one night there without Daddy. My state of aloneness made me uneasy; there were no double dead-bolt locks or alarm system to make me feel more secure and no deer rifle in the gun rack. I tucked the pepper spray I'd brought under the mattress and poured myself another glass of wine. I can do this, I kept telling myself.

The vapor lamp outside had long since burned out. As darkness filled each window of the cabin, I secured the chain on the entry door, pulled all the shades down tight and slipped under the blanket on the double bed, stacking the pillows behind me as I phoned Dan, his voice warming the cockles of my heart, but little else.

The last time I'd talked to Daddy, all the usual starch had gone from his voice. He'd reluctantly given up the keys to his Suburban after running through a barbed wire fence, obsessing about not having any wheels. Sensing his loneliness, I extended another invitation to him to spend half the year in North Carolina with us, but he wouldn't budge. He was right where he wanted to be, back where his life began. The same feeling of loneliness and isolation surged through me as I bid my husband good night and flipped from channel to channel looking for something to take my mind off Daddy and the cold, dank room that was to be my home for five days.

I woke up early the next morning to the high-lonesome sound of a coyote in the lower pasture. The temperature inside the cabin hadn't budged even one degree, and I cursed the time I'd taken and money I'd spent on the worthless radiator. I rooted around in the medicine cabinet for some aspirin to soothe my wine headache, found Daddy's partial plate, and dropped it into a paper cup to soak, wondering if he'd ever wear it again.

I opened the lid to the coffeemaker and found moldy coffee grounds inside, remembering that Daddy had taken a spill on his way from the bathroom to the kitchenette early on that fateful December morning, an image I couldn't erase from my mind. Ben said he'd probably tripped over a shoelace, ripping the telephone cord from the wall trying to get help, that he always checked on him by eight o'clock each morning and found him on the floor in excruciating pain. He'd bought him the infamous pair of tennis shoes when he could no longer manage his boots, regretting the decision.

I dumped out the old grounds and started a new pot, glancing up at the wall calendar above the sink where Dad had outlined each day in December with a red marker so he could see them better. I poured myself a cup of black coffee and sat next to the pine cabinet waiting for the aspirin to kick in. Like so much of the furniture we'd grown up with, Daddy made the pine cabinet in his workshop. A civil engineer by trade, he'd always been a tireless tinker, cabinetmaker, and jack-of-all-trades, never stopping for much of anything. And without Mother to pick up after him, the remnants of his everyday life were scattered across its surface: paper clips, pencils, coffee-stained cups, junk mail, rubber bands, corn pads, foot powder.

I missed the days when Daddy walked through the cabin sure-footed, sighing in happy contentment, humming a soft "Ho, ho, ho" as he passed through. And I missed sitting out on the sun porch with him, a flurry of white plats spread across his work table as he drew up a survey. That they were all land surveys on properties that heirs either wanted to divide or sell didn't bother him in the least, though sooner or later he'd come up with a story about the good old days working in the Gulf.

"I was riding a helicopter to an offshore rig one day and we were having a heck of a time finding it. Finally, the pilot shouted that if we didn't find the rig in fifteen minutes we'd have to head back, that he was almost out of fuel."

The sun room—which had been a screened-in porch before Dad converted it years ago, installing jalousies and plate-glass windows all around—was a pleasant place to sit and watch the world go by. But it was too frigid without the sun's rays coming through the glass, and the fact there was no propane for the gas logs he'd installed didn't help.

I sorted through a small stack of papers and old bills on the cabinet, studying the weather page from the *Austin-American Statesman*. Again, he'd marked above each day of the week, 14, 15, 16, 17, 18, and so on across the top of the page, circling Saturday with a notation that read: Ben gone to Hou and back. I puzzled over the meaning of Hou. Did he mean the house or Houston? It was an August paper. That would have been right after our visit, making it obvious to me that he was trying desperately to hold onto his memory, the hours ticking by for him in a desolate string of days.

Daddy's dementia began in fits and starts beginning with the TV remote. From one visit to the next, he just couldn't grasp how to work the remote, and no amount of coaching or written instructions seemed to help. Then he lost his cell phone and couldn't figure out the new one. These lapses were hard to accept coming from someone whose mind had once been sharp as a snake's tooth. I remember when he started marking dates on the eggs in the fridge in pencil, but never gave it much thought. It seemed like the kind of thing a detail person, someone whose life has been all about precision, would do.

During our August visit in 2010 to celebrate his ninetieth birthday, he seemed all- consumed about the correct time. After I checked my cell phone and moved the long hand, he taped a tiny note at the base of the wall clock that read "Correct time." The day of the party, friends and family from across the state gathered at the ranch for a barbecue. Although he didn't recognize any of them, it never dampened anyone's enthusiasm to celebrate, even when the outdoor thermometer read 103.

It disturbed me greatly that he didn't recognize his cousin Peggy, my great-uncle Pomp's daughter. They'd always been close, but no matter how hard she tried, she couldn't unlock memory's chamber. The same went for Peggy's son—my second cousin, Mark—another of Dad's protégés who's become a talented and sought-after luthier out in Oregon. Mark developed a love for woodworking through time spent with Dad in his workshop. His talent has taken him far and wide. Coca-Cola even commissioned him to make a ukulele for Warren Buffett.

When we gathered around the picnic table at the pond, Mark at his side, I asked Dad how it felt to be ninety years old. Suddenly, he seemed like his old self again, full of vinegar when he paused reflectively and smiled, "Well, I thought I'd feel a whole lot worse."

One of the last times we talked on the phone, Dad asked me who all had come to his funeral, then paused, correcting himself. "I meant to say party," he laughed. "It's about the same thing." I drove back to the nursing home mid-morning, thawing out in the warmth of the rental car. Patches, the resident dog, a speckled white boxer with a big brown patch over one eye, was roaming the halls, adding a touch of normalcy to a place Daddy once jokingly called a "halfway house, a place of transition between the "here and the hereafter."

When I stepped into his room, a flicker of recognition crossed his face. He mumbled something I couldn't make out, rubbing his nose and tugging at one ear in frustration. Because he couldn't take food or water, the nurses had to swab his mouth periodically, so I pulled the wrapper off a tiny stick-sponge that reminded me of a Popsicle, wet it with some special mouthwash, and gingerly cleaned the funk from his mouth. After I finished, he started working his tongue in an effort to speak.

"I've been out in the field," he said in a subdued tone I'd become accustomed to.

"Really?" I smiled.

Before he retired from Amoco, he staked oil wells and repositioned rigs all over the state. For someone so active, it must have been a nightmare being bedridden and helpless as a newborn. As I drew the curtain back to show him the fine mist coating the windowpane, he raised one limp arm into the air, drawing his hand back as though pulling something from a shelf.

"What are you doing, Daddy?" I asked after he did this repeatedly with both hands.

"I'm getting some transparencies," he said, likely referring to some step in the outmoded form of drafting that's been replaced by CAD on a computer.

"What are transparencies, Daddy?"

"It's something you can't see," he explained. "I'm getting you three or four."

I said "okay" and hung around awhile longer. He was in his own little world. And content to be there. After he nodded off, I returned to the cabin to box up the radiator and eat a bite before driving the twenty miles back to Bastrop, passing the familiar turnoff to Woods Fort, another one of those obscure places Dad discovered years ago while out surveying; there was nothing he liked better than logging mile after mile through the Texas countryside. When he got rid of his Colony Park, the odometer reading was 350,000 miles—on the same transmission and the same transmission fluid. The day we drove together to see Woods Fort, I expected to see the fort in all its glory. After the big buildup, I was a bit deflated when we pulled up to a historical marker and a magnificent stand of prickly pear cactus where the fort once stood. That evening, I treated Ben to supper at the Guadalajara, and we discussed Daddy's progress over frosty bottles of Dos Equis—what Medicare would pay for and how much money he had in the bank—before turning to more pleasant topics, such as the recent graduation of his younger son from the University of Houston; visits to see his two grandchildren in Galveston; hunting trips with my two nephews.

"We spotted fifteen wild turkeys in the lower pasture a couple of weeks ago," he said with sudden enthusiasm. "Six were nesting in one of the deer blinds. They gave Taylor quite a scare when he climbed up there and spooked 'em," he chuckled.

The days crawled by for me, each one as raw and foreboding as the day before. The nurse said Daddy had his days and nights mixed up, so I never knew when I'd find him awake. To fill in around my visits, I weeded out the cabin, tossing a broken hairdryer into the trash, along with boxes of crackers and canned goods long past their sell-by dates. After he turned ninety, Dad said he wanted to make it to a hundred. But the empty vodka bottle and a six-pack of Five Hour Energy drink told the whole story. He'd been running out of steam physically for some time. The vodka must have soothed his mind while the energy drink may or may not have given him a boost.

I spent all the money I'd gotten back on the radiator on cleaning supplies at the Dollar General, sprucing up the cabin a little more. I did uncover a small ceramic heater that worked like a charm, though the breaker blew when I used the microwave, so I had to use caution. It wasn't until I decided to tackle the pine cabinet that I ran across a large brown envelope with my name printed neatly across the front in Daddy's precise hand. Its top riddled by silverfish, the envelope contained a time capsule of our lives. Tucked inside were Father's Day cards and birthday cards we'd given him as children, along with a couple of yellowed postcards we'd mailed him from Rhode Island while visiting Mom's family. One postcard was a sliver of my girlhood, and as I read it, I saw myself at the age of twelve:

> *"Dear Daddy, The plane trip was just as exciting as flying to the moon. It was a beautiful night for flying. Gramma fixed up our room real nice. Benjie, Mother and I are all fine and rested. Wish you were here with us. Love, Susan."*

I pictured Daddy smiling as he read it. I saw him phoning his mother and reading it to her as a laugh track went off in my head. I saw him driving our gray Plymouth Savoy from Texas to Providence, four days alone on the road to pick us up. And I saw Gram Follett giving us bars of soap to use on the trip back instead of those tiny motel soaps. Funny how one little postcard could open memory's gate. And if I hadn't been cleaning, I never would have found it.

I run a duster over a table lamp and a bowl of motel soaps sitting on the small bookcase in the bunk room, lingering over his old Argus 8mm movie camera, still in its original leather case, pulling out a bulky letter wedged between some books, the envelope marked "High Island" in Dad's hand. The return address is that of a woman from Austin; a handwritten note inside thanks him for tackling such an onerous job, enclosing a check and some pictures. High Island, a bird sanctuary and rookery on the Texas coast, had always been a place dear to his heart.

I flip through the snapshots from his survey job on the Biglin Marsh: Dad and crew slogging through the mud flats; a mud-buggy with gigantic wheels to get through the swampy areas on the sound; a member of the crew holding a dead water moccasin on the end of a stick; a sand-hill crane in flight, pastel pink against a powder-blue sky; Dad in a red jacket and ball cap, having the time of his life manning a john boat with a broad, toothy smile.

Just when I thought I might blow my brains out because of the dreary weather and my anxiety about Daddy, two of my cousins arrived from

Houston. I felt the heavens opening up as Pam and Lauran filed into the cabin carrying bags of food: small tubs of deli items, boxes of salty snacks, my favorite HEB coffee, a Whitman's Sampler, and two pounds of fresh Gulf shrimp. They treated me to lunch at a small bistro on the town square, and I relished the laughter and woman-song that lit up our table between bites of tossed salad, crawfish bisque, and hot yeast rolls. We drove to the nursing home after lunch to see Daddy, but we could have been the Dixie Chicks for all he knew, his discomfort apparent when he reverted back to the ear-tugging and nose-scratching.

Before heading back to Houston, my cousins made me promise to call if I needed anything or just wanted to vent. Oh, how I hated seeing them go. That evening, Ben grilled the shrimp on bamboo skewers and I carried tubs of potato salad and macaroni salad over to the house. That Daddy didn't seem to be making any progress was written all over his face when we sat down at my grandmother's claw-foot dining table.

"I'd like to see him eating something," he said with some resignation between bites of food. "I'd like to see him out on the riding mower again. I patched the tires. They were full of mesquite thorns."

"I'd like to see him pop the top on a Miller Lite again," I added.

We ate in stony silence for a while before the conversation turned again to Dad's expenses, his recovery dragging on much longer than we'd expected. If there was to be a recovery, a subject I cautiously avoided.

"The nursing home charges a hundred and thirty dollars a day," Ben said. "Do the math. When Medicare runs out, what's coming in won't cover it. I've got the director looking into whether he's eligible for any military benefits."

"He doesn't have a pot to pee in or a window to throw it out of, so the saying goes," I said, my words hanging in the air, things left unsaid: how an intelligent man like our father could have gone so astray after Mom died, the reckless spending, the careless disregard for the future, how he hadn't saved anything for a rainy day. By the same token, he'd been the center of our universe; he was a good father, a good provider, steady as they come. I kept my rage buried deep. After all is said and done, the good times kept rising to the top like a dollop of sweet cream.

On Monday morning, Daddy seemed to have turned a corner. The minute I walked into his room, he pointed to me and said, "I know you. You're Susan Perry."

Propped up in bed reading the local paper, he pointed to an ad for his bank and read it aloud. Ben was all smiles, visiting with the physical therapist in the hallway. For the first time since my arrival, I felt giddy with joy. I stayed longer than usual, watching as an aide hoisted my father, fragile as a China doll, into a chair using a sling and a hydraulic lift. Alarmingly, after she positioned him in the chair, he wilted like a hothouse flower.

"His blood pressure just dropped," she explained, "but he'll come around."

As he perked up, she handed him a warm wash cloth and he began wiping his face. He went back to reading the paper and I stayed until he dropped off to sleep in the chair. Late that afternoon, overcome with cabin fever, I decided to drive to the outskirts of Houston to visit my friend Kay. Though a twinge of guilt gnawed at me as I packed a few things for the trip, my cousin's words—take care of yourself—kept repeating I needed a diversion, a female voice, more of the woman-song I'd enjoyed two days earlier. Kay and her husband had recently moved to a new gated community in Cypress. And I so wanted to see the house but never seemed to find the time. Kay and Daddy have been kindred spirits going back to the 1970's when we first struck up a friendship. She's spent a lot of time at the ranch, and I felt I'd neglected a friend who's always dropped everything to come to me.

The sun was beginning to peek out from behind the clouds as I pulled into the driveway of their brick hacienda out on the prairie. I heaved a big sigh of relief seeing Kay standing in the doorway, welcoming me with her usual hug. At a time when most of my friends are downsizing, Kay and her husband opted for rooms spacious enough to house small armies, granite countertops the size of landing strips, and walk-in closets Imelda Marcos would envy. Our voices echoing off the tile floors as Kay gave me the grand tour.

After lunch, we took a leisurely walk on the hiking trails that wound through a series of lakes, Kay's bubbly personality like a tonic, all my cares melting away as we rounded the last curve and made our way back to the house. But as soon as we stepped inside the door my cell phone rang, my brother's name flashing across the screen.

"The nursing home called and said Dad's non-responsive," he said. "They're taking him to the emergency room now."

I cut my visit short, heading for the super-slab that would take me to the Austin Bypass, driving on pure adrenalin and mentally kicking myself for my indulgence. "You can't hit the rewind button once they're gone," a friend once said. The whole purpose of my visit was to come to Dad's emotional rescue, and I felt I'd done a miserable job.

It was growing dark by the time I pulled up to St. Mark's. Ben looked like he'd been hit by a bus and run over by several cars as he sank into a chair beside me in the waiting room, trying to explain a situation that really had no explanation.

"Are you hungry?" I asked, not knowing what else to say.

He gave me a dazed look and I told him to go on home. One meltdown between us was enough for one day. An attendant led me through the double doors and on to Daddy's bed, his hands so cold they might have been chipped from the polar ice cap. I gave them a gentle squeeze and introduced myself to the attending physician, a short man with blondish hair and gentle blue eyes who looked to be my age.

While a nurse checked Dad's vital signs, we moved outside to the corridor and he began to talk.

"These seniors who break hips, well, it's hard to say what's going to happen," he said, sounding like he was holding back, measuring his words before he spoke. "I think I remember him. He was here for the hip surgery. When we told him he needed a hip replacement, he said he wanted to go home and think it over," he grinned.

"Then we sent him to Brackenridge in Austin to treat the pneumonia," he continued, "probably from lying on a cold floor too long. Then back here to a nursing home. Then back to Austin with colitis. Yeah. It's rough when they get his age," he repeated. "Hard to say..." he trailed off, scratching his head and leaving the unspoken words hanging between us like dirty laundry.

"My father's never been a quitter," I smiled.

"Well, his blood pressure dropped over at the home. They probably kept him up in a chair too long. We'll keep him here a day or two until he's stable."

I stayed with Daddy until he fell asleep, then drove back to the cabin and collapsed. Is this the way he's going to go out, I kept thinking, with one final gasp of normalcy before the last hurrah? That night I dreamed about Daddy. He was sitting in that sling, suspended out over a dark abyss. I kept trying to reach him, to drag him to safety, but no matter how hard I tried, I couldn't do anything to help him. He just kept slipping deeper and deeper into the abyss, mere inches from my fingertips. When I clawed my way out of a wine-induced sleep, my rational mind took over. The dream spoke to my helplessness since his accident, and everything that had gone on before.

I bought some colorful helium balloons in the gift shop early the next morning and spent my last full day at the hospital with Daddy. As the food carts went rattling down the hallway, filling his room with breakfast aromas, he asked me to get him a cup of coffee.

It broke my heart to deny him that small pleasure, but the nurse had cautioned me that he might aspirate, and I didn't dare take a chance, confident that he was in good hands as I watched nurses and therapists and aides of every description hover over him throughout the day.

Just when I'd be back wasn't clear, but I had the cabin spotless by the time I left, the sun shining through the windowpanes, all traces of gray mist burned away. I had a voicemail from Kay, something to the effect that if I needed her help with funeral arrangements to give her a call. I ignored the message, tossing my phone aside as the ranch slid away behind me. I couldn't bring myself to call her back. If I did, I'd have to face the truth. And the truth is something I can't see. ❧

Daddy with a dead rattler on a survey in South Texas

Chapter 17 – Endings And Beginnings

If you must talk about the weather, someone said to me,
Please—no rain resembling tears,
No sun as fiery orb,
No silken breezes either.

— TEXAS POETRY CALENDAR 2015 BY STEPHANIE MADAN

We flew to Texas on St. Patrick's Day, a sunny spring day in the Carolinas, with rain expected in Houston and at the ranch as a front moved through. I hadn't been back to the Blue Branch since Dad died on Easter Sunday, 2011, five years before, the longest stretch of time that I'd ever been away. I guess it had taken me that long to face a visit knowing he wouldn't be there. But after twenty-plus years of back and forth, racing through airports to make a connection, I needed a break.

Our seats were located over the wing, which surprised me since I'd never chosen our seating to begin with. Daddy used to say the safest seats on an airplane are over the wing, and a good flight is one you can walk away from, a throwback to his Air Force training during WWII, a thought that made me smile. We picked up our rental car and drove

173

the backroads from the Houston airport in hopes of spotting some bluebonnets along the way. By the time we reached Brenham, we saw some pretty patches here and there, but I'd seen better in years past, thinking about how the rain has to come at just the right time, and what a finicky flower a bluebonnet can be.

After a tedious drive behind some gawkers in Round Top, where we passed antique dealers setting up for the festival (but zero flowers), we pulled into the ranch in late afternoon, driving the rutted gravel road gingerly to avoid dings, the Kiger place to the other side of the barbed wire fence deserted but for the cattle since Mrs. Kiger moved to Austin and put it up for sale. I'd seen the listing on the Internet, an astronomical asking price she'll be lucky to get with the downturn in oil prices. And if she does get it, it doesn't bode well for my brother's property taxes.

Several pair of Ben's jeans hung on a clothesline out back as we approached the house. Dressed in a pair of frayed Bermuda shorts and canvas deck shoes, a ball cap mashed down over a shock of graying hair, he came through the back door to meet us. The rain had bypassed us, a brisk wind whipping at our clothes as we hugged and sat on some lawn chairs under a pecan tree, the grass a brilliant green as far as the eye could see, the wild grasses in the upper pasture bowing in the distance.

I would have preferred the cabin to the motel room we'd reserved in town but felt uneasy about the shape I'd find it in, not to mention the frost warning and lack of heat therein. Ben had had a run of bad luck after renting it out, assuring me during a phone call that he'd painted all the rooms and hung new blinds prior to his son Taylor's wedding reception and he was done with renters. Though I knew the cabin wouldn't be as we left it after Dad's service, in my mind it still looked the same, file cabinets stuffed with surveys in each corner of the sun porch, antique tools neatly hung around the windows, Dad's clothes hanging on a rack in the bunk room, framed pictures of him on the dresser, still ruggedly handsome at ninety, a blue wash bowl and pitcher, an old family piece, sitting alongside a smaller bowl heaped with tiny motel soaps he'd collected during his travels.

I'd been a little disappointed about the sparse bluebonnet display, but felt rejuvenated just the same, the smell of cut grass tickling all my senses. The happy times always seem to take over when you least expect them to, an enchantment in the lichen-covered limbs of the live oaks, the resurrection ferns just coming to life at the pond. T.S. Elliott said we all end up where we started. And know the place for the first time. I'd save my pilgrimage to the blue hole for later.

Dan was so happy to be back in the Brisket Belt that he repeated his mantra about eating brisket every day as we got caught up over a few beers, Ben waxing poetic about the new chicken coop his kids had given him for Christmas, although there were no baby chicks for sale until April. I was delighted to learn that my two nephews were coming for the weekend, the cedar coop they'd given Ben for Christmas more a rustic dollhouse painted a cocoa brown. My brother was in rare form, an explosion of words, anxious to tell us about his day-to-day life. Frankly, I don't know how he does it. Living alone day in and day out might send me over the edge.

As we stood around the coop, Ben said he missed Aunt Edna's yard eggs and those rich orange yolks. Filtering down to an eerie scene from the past, he relived the day he and Cathy returned from town to find their entire flock of Araucana hens splayed out in the yard, no presence of blood or bullet wounds, their necks broken, a mystery until two of Uncle Fred's dogs appeared from behind the barn. Fred and Sue loved their dogs. (I remember a toy poodle named Twister that Fred carried in the cook of his arm everywhere he went.) A quick phone call and Fred appeared, his eyes glazed over as he stepped out of his pickup with a rifle, perhaps a shot of Wild Turkey for courage before pulling the trigger, a Lucky Strike afterward to take some of the edge off, a heartbreaker all the way around.

The large vegetable garden Dad always filled with okra, purple hulls, squash, collards, and all things vegetable was slam full of Johnson grass, the deer winning that battle. Bluebird houses dotted the landscape as Ben pointed out the small garden at the old kitchen he'd filled with cabbage plants, broccoli, and asparagus. He'd positioned it close to the house where deer never tread, two wrens dipping into a lavender bush at a corner of the house as he spoke. He'd planted an herb bed that ran along a sidewalk at the back porch, nurturing all living things after a long hiatus.

At some point, my curiosity took over, and I proceeded to the cabin, leaving the men to their conversations about home brewing, how to remove an enormous snapping turtle that's taken over the swimming hole…managing a bee hive…checking the supers on his bee hives… catching swarms in the springtime fading in the wind at my back as I left. A smattering of scarlet sage that puts a ring of fire around the barn each spring brought a smile to my face as I approached the cabin.

Who is it that said he who hesitates is lost? I'd seen the cabin as we pulled in, the casement window frames painted cobalt blue. They stood out like neon signs against the white lap siding, giving the cabin a garish look. But a flower garden to either side of the entry door with its rock border and a rose bush in bud took some of the edge off, bringing to mind an English country cottage.

I stepped onto the porch ready to see dingy plate-glass windows and jalousies soiled from the constant smoke roiling from passing trains, surprised to find them immaculate. The slate had been wiped clean, the sun porch cleared of everything save a card table and four chairs at its center, a bookcase behind the door, and Dad's red cone-shaped fireplace, the brick-red floor so clean it looked as though it had been given a fresh coat of paint, the knotty pine paneling under the windows fresh and alive.

The cabin door was another story. No longer white, a previous tenant had painted the sashing black and black, the four panels a deep purple with a white border as if the old door was trying desperately to get out, the only consolation the porcelain door knob still intact. I pushed through to find an absence of clutter, an open, airy room with an overstuffed ivory loveseat in one corner, a double bed I recognized as one of Granny's in the other, the walls painted a soft white. A large braided rug dominated the room, a racetrack of green, white and burgundy, the stove and mini-fridge gone. How many bowls of potato salad had I shoved into that fridge? How many gallons of chili had I cooked on that rusty old stove? I breathed a sigh of relief when I saw my grandmother's kitchen chairs at the drop-down table, the ones I'd painted deep blue eons ago, still blue! I opened a few cabinets on the kitchenette. No sticky traps, no varmints anywhere.

The bunk room had been pared down to the bare essentials. A twin bed, a dresser painted to match the front door, a small bedside table I recognized as one of my grandmother's, mercifully untouched. The linoleum in the bathroom had been replaced with a white tile floor, the shower stall along with the commode clean and tidy, a fresh roll of toilet tissue at my disposal.

After Daddy died, I always assumed I'd return again surrounded by all of his things, another time to reflect and to grieve, to breathe in his essence, a time to laugh or cry, or cut loose with a primal scream. A time to remember and a time to forget. I thought I'd leave feeling lower than a slimy river bottom, but as I walked back through the rooms, pausing to take it all in, I had to admit that I liked the simplicity of it, the cabin stripped down to its bare bones once again.

I sat on the sun porch, meditating and ruminating. When you laugh, the world laughs with you. When you cry, you cry alone. I was glad to be out of the wind for a while, but the tears weren't coming. In some ways, Daddy's death had been a relief—a release from the constant worry as he was shuffled from one facility to another, from skilled care to acute care, from town to town, from La Grange to Luling to Schulenburg to Giddings as he stumbled deeper and deeper into the dark pit of dementia, down to his last collar button in the end, my carry-on bag always packed and at the ready, the relentless stress as I flew back and forth. Even so, I miss him terribly. How could I not? Despite his many setbacks, he'd hoped to make it to a hundred, his voice faint as a mouse's squeak as he told the nurse in ICU, "This is my daughter."

This is my daughter will abide in my heart forever.

When he died, it was as if someone had turned off all the lights. Dark for all of us as we filtered through our loss, our grief, our brains short-circuited as we tried to make arrangements that felt monumental. A month to the day after Daddy died, he came to me in a dream. We were in the cabin. I was making coffee. He was smiling, telling me a funny story. He looked healthy, much younger, maybe in his sixties, shaking his hips in the telling, though I can't say what it was about, just a happy, intimate moment between the two of us.

I thought about the toast we made to Ivan after the service, passing around a six pack of Miller Lite. I thought about how a gust of wind had picked up the flower arrangement I'd set on the sill by the jalousies, flipping it end over end, and the improbability of it landing at my feet, upright on the concrete floor without spilling a drop of water or disturbing the flowers. I thought about the door to Dad's old bedroom swinging open on its own, once, twice, three times while we sat in the big house eating supper, thinking our private thoughts, a dark shadow falling across the table as Taylor jumped up to close it each time. I thought about the pack of coyotes that gathered below the railroad tracks that evening, and how their mournful cries made my skin crawl. And Kerry's phone call from Boulder a week later when he said he'd been surfing on the Colorado River, and how he'd grabbed a vintage can of Miller Lite floating past him, unopened, the old ring tab still in place. I knew then that Dad's spirit was ethereal, far-reaching and timeless.

We were sitting under the pecan tree out back when my cousin Pam pulled in on Friday and parked her bright red Passat next to the cabin. The last time we'd been together at the Blue Branch we were driving through town, visiting and reveling in a song from the Rosanne Cash CD, *Black Cadillac*. Then I got pulled over for speeding past the high school. I rolled down my window and pulled out my driver's license, handing it to the young woman officer. She made a remark about my being from North Carolina and asked me why I'd been speeding. I told her that I was there to visit my 90-year-old father in a nursing home in Giddings, and that I'd been rear-ended on my way there from the airport and had to await the police and another rental car, basically a sob story, but all true. She gave me an apologetic look and said to be more careful in the future, waving us on. As we pulled away, Pam giggled, "Good one, Susan. I'll have to remember that one."

We dropped Ben off at the Blue Branch after a brisket lunch at the Back Porch and drove to City Cemetery where a solid carpet of bluebonnets greeted us, the gray granite headstones set adrift in a sea of blue. We parked under a sprawling oak tree at the Perry plot and stepped out. It was the first I'd seen of Daddy's stone, the one the Army provided with a simple cross above his name, Ivan W. Perry, PFC US Army, World War II and the dates, all etched in black.

An American stick flag fluttering in the wind took me back to the day of his service. A gale force wind had kicked up, the flower arrangements toppling over at every turn, the wind threatening to rip the graveside tent right off its moorings. A straw cowgirl hat with a chin strap anchored my hair down as I read the eulogy I'd written. With grit blowing all around us and rattling my pages, I was miles from nowhere as I spoke at the top of my game to be heard.

Ben read a passage from the Bible that came about in the form of an epiphany after Daddy died. He'd been sitting under the pecan tree, grieving like we all were, when a twig fell into his pocket. He had an appointment that day with a man named John at the funeral home and pulled out the family Bible, turning to the Gospel According to Saint John, Chapter 15: "I am the true vine, and my Father is the husbandman. Every branch in me that beareth not fruit be taken away: and every branch that beareth fruit, he purgeth it, that it may bring forth more fruit." Pam helped me plan the service, and somehow, we'd gotten through it, hitting the high points of his life, a life sprinkled with humor that became humorous tales later on.

When we were kids, we bought a Chihuahua pup named Paco based on a recent newspaper article that stated Chihuahuas cured asthma. Not only did he not cure my brother's asthma, he barked incessantly, bit the mailman on several occasions, and wouldn't touch dog food. Mother fried up a hamburger patty for Paco each morning and he slept between my parents at night, snarling if my dad got too close, Mother so attached by this point that disposing of him wasn't an option. We took him with us everywhere. He'd been to Rhode Island and back several times. He had a bad habit of lifting his leg on the furniture, so relatives were always glad to see him go. We'd sneak him into motel rooms and get puzzled looks at burger joints when Dad ordered a hamburger patty without the bun.

One evening some family friends called long distance. They'd had car trouble somewhere out west and needed money to get home. Dad said he'd wire them some cash by Western Union and a while later the Western Union operator called back and instructed Dad to ask them some question that only they could answer. It only took Dad a split second to reply: "What's the name of the smartest dog in the whole world?"

As we turned to leave, I was surprised to see Jim Kiger's headstone only yards away from Daddy's. A double stone with Mary's name and birth date. I'd almost missed it and found it fitting that Dad and his old friend are resting so close to each other.

We moved on into town, parking at the courthouse, the centerpiece of the town square. A three-story Romanesque Revival, it's built of native stone: blue sandstone from Muldoon trimmed with red Pecos sandstone, pink Burnet granite, and white Belton limestone. It's one of my favorite buildings, from the twelve chimneys to the clock tower to the gargoyles sitting sentinel at each peak. After taking some pictures in the adjacent flower garden, we hit a few of the shops where I added to my stock of sympathy cards at the Hallmark, touring the new Texas Quilt Museum before returning to the Blue Branch mid-afternoon.

Taylor had just put a carton of Shiner beer into an orange cooler, dumping in a bag of ice as we approached. His wife, Annie, also a teacher, couldn't make it due to a school project. We had to miss their wedding at one of the painted churches outside of Schulenburg because my father-in-law's health was failing at the time, his death imminent. When Taylor said he had a surprise, I immediately thought Annie might be expecting, my head spinning with anticipation. Instead, he led us to the front yard where he'd killed a sizeable water moccasin, splayed out on the flagstone walk.

"I almost stepped on it. It was sunning on the grass," he said, bumping out his chest with pride.

When I look at him all grown up, married and teaching fifth grade, I still see the young boy riding his tricycle down the hill to the creek, the teenager who aced his SATs but wanted to work on Daddy's survey crew instead of going to college. We had some catching up to do over a few beers.

We ate a Tex-Mex supper at the Guadalajara, ordering frozen Margaritas and a smattering of everything on the menu, it seemed, Taylor so like Cathy, talkative and witty, his mind always churning, always looking for new ways to engage his students, taking in the world at a frantic pace. Years ago, he'd been working on a novel, something about zombies or vampires, I forget which. When he picked up the check, I handed him a twenty, ever the doting aunt who won't let him be grown up.

Pam had booked a room at our motel and followed us through town and across the Colorado River Bridge. That night in our room, silently scrolling through our smart phones, I found a voicemail from Cathy. She and Steve were heading to Austin to visit a friend, wondering if we could meet somewhere for lunch, and I sent her a text. Somehow, we've remained friends through the years though it didn't come easily after she and Ben divorced, evolving over time.

I felt especially flattered the year she and Steve stopped off for a weekend visit during a road trip to New York. She said her bucket list included seeing where we lived and making a sojourn to the town of Lucama, North Carolina, to see the Vollis Simpson Whirligig Park. I'd never been to Lucama, though it was just a short drive away. In anticipation of their arrival, I stocked up on local sausage and pork barbecue only to find out she'd turned vegetarian. This sudden reversal came by way of a dream that told her she could only eat what she could kill. She said that she might be capable of killing a fish.

Cathy and my father had remained close through various projects at the ranch and the lot surveys she sent his way. When she wished him a happy birthday at his party, he gave her a blank stare.

"Do I know you?" he asked, a thing he used to say in jest whenever I called.

She sat with him for a while, patiently tossing memories into the air like a game of charades (mother to his grandkids, the lot surveys) until he perked up in total recall, his smile bright and welcoming.

"Oh! Cathy! Of course! Cathy!"

She was the only person he recognized that day besides me, Kerry, Ben, and my nephews. And how could I forget the weekend I almost got stranded at the ranch? When it came time for Dad to drive me back to Houston to catch my flight, he reluctantly declined. No Hertz or Enterprise car rentals in a small town like La Grange. What to do? Then, in the eleventh hour, understanding my plight, Cathy came to my rescue, making the trek from Houston to fetch me.

I value her friendship hugely and owe her a great cosmic debt for looking after Dad when I couldn't. She knew about our trip, but a family gathering at the ranch just wasn't in the cards, in good spirits when I called back, still determined to see me. She'd call again on their way back to Houston to see what suited. God bless her gypsy soul.

Nephew Benjie was due early Saturday morning, so after picking up cheese kolaches and coffee at Weikel's Bakery, then some sticky buns at Lukas Bakery, we set out for the Blue Branch. The kitchen looked nice. Ben had finally finished the bead board wall at the sink area and installed the counter cabinets. A gaping space at one end spoke of a dishwasher yet to come. He'd already made English muffins with eggs, bacon and cheese, still on the stove in anticipation of Benjie and his girlfriend who were running late. As I bit into a kolache, still warm and yeasty and delectable, I noticed my mother's old battered and splattered recipe box on a shelf in the pantry. Stuffed with 3x5 index cards—neatly typed on her powder blue Smith Corona, a gift from Daddy—along with clippings Dad cut from the newspaper, it brought back memories of the New England clam chowder, or "chowda," she used to make on cold winter nights.

Ben said they had supper under control. He planned to smoke some ribs, venison sausage. and a pork roast, a craft he learned at Dad's elbow. Taylor said he'd be making garlic mashed potatoes, cheesy French bread, and slaw. A German chocolate sheet cake sat cooling on the kitchen table in anticipation of Benjie's birthday, which I'd forgotten about completely.

We decided to drive to Monument Hill mid-morning to hike the trails, the wind still whipping incessantly as we made our way to the tomb where seventeen "Texians" are interred, the ones captured and executed by Santa Ana in the Black Bean Death Lottery, the massive granite vault placed over the old decaying tomb and re-dedicated in 1936, the centennial of Texas independence. The monument, a forty-eight-foot obelisk of native stone, towers over them with colored panels depicting the drawing of the beans. A bronze angel holding a sword at its base watches over them. La Grange was chosen for their final resting place because it had been the home of Captain William Eastland, the only officer executed in the Black Bean Incident. His epitaph reads: Greater love hath no man than this—that a man lay down his life for his friends. Hallowed ground.

I stood there thinking about one of Dad's bedtime stories, about the time, on a dare, he spent the night atop the old cracked and crumbling tomb. He could hardly sleep under the glare of a full moon, imagining ghosts as owls hooted all around. After a few pictures, we took in the view of the Colorado River some two hundred feet below us, the town proper transformed into something you'd see in a miniature train set, the landscape a patchwork of green and gold that fanned out to the blue horizon. The lantana was in full bloom along the trails as we made our way past the old Kreische family homestead. Heinrich, a master stonemason and German immigrant, built the three-story stone house for his wife and six children, adding a brewery in a deep ravine behind the house in 1860. When a batch of his Bluff Beer was ready, he'd raise a flag that read: Frisch Auf, which means Freshen Up.

We drove back to the Back Porch for lunch, savoring the brisket, pinto beans, and slaw. I was eating the last tender, smoky bite, about to go into a food coma, when Cathy sent me a text. They were ten minutes away. Dan begged off. He wouldn't miss Duke basketball come hell or high water and returned to the motel. It was March Madness, after all. Pam and I fought to get a parking space near Latte on The Square, the town square jumping with traffic as some local wineries were setting up for an afternoon tasting, Cathy waving to us from a table at the far corner of the coffee shop.

"Order whatever you like," Steve smiled as we approached. "It's on me."

I wasn't the least bit hungry but couldn't resist a scoop of butter pecan ice cream from the Blue Bell freezer.

"We have fifteen minutes to visit," Cathy grinned, sprigs of her blond hair peeking out from a white ball cap embellished with multi-colored stones. "We're picking up Tish at the Houston airport later," she added, referring to her childhood friend.

When I admired her ball cap, she said she'd had a melanoma removed from her scalp. "That's what happens when you have thinning hair in Texas. They assured me they got it all," she grinned while Steve quietly worked his way to the bottom of a mug of raisin oatmeal.

Cathy wanted to know if I'd been to the Bugle Boy, a listening room in town. Trout Fishing in America, one of her favorite bands, was slated to play there.

"How are y'all doing?" she asked cheerfully, glancing Pam's way.

While Pam filled Cathy in about her hearing loss and recent cataract surgery, I thought back to the first time we shaved our legs, giggling together behind Granny's bathroom door, our youth just vapor now, coming to as Cathy turned to me for a report.

"Tendonitis, arthritis, overactive bladder, acid reflux, and bunions," I replied, jokingly. "From here on out, it's all about the maintenance."

"You forgot osteoporosis," Pam chimed in, grinning.

Cathy giggled before turning serious. "We were in Austin visiting a friend with terminal cancer. He doesn't have much longer. It's very sad," she said with a downcast look.

A short silence consumed the table. At our age, the passing of friends and family members brings our mortality to the forefront. And this includes celebrities and rock stars. David Bowie, my age, had died six weeks before. Cancer, heart attacks, strokes, Alzheimer's—the losses an abomination. And at a certain age you start culling through the obits each morning, paying attention to the age brackets, reading the obits of complete strangers as step by querulous step you move a little closer to the precipice, depending on how long God gives you, if you happen to believe in a god, death becoming palpable—a nagging presence, a thing you hadn't bargained for in your youth.

"I realized I'd turned a corner when my hairdresser started calling me Miss Susan," I added in all seriousness. "She does a pretty good job of putting new hair on an aging face though."

Cathy giggled, and Steve, the only rooster at a hen party, grinned at me broadly. "How was the ice cream?"

"Hit the spot," I said. "Cholesterol and listeria be damned!"

And with that, we all rose from the table. Our fifteen minutes were up.

I paused on the sidewalk, waving goodbye, and reeling in the years as their Prius disappeared into the traffic, riffs from Steely Dan and the Eagles spinning through my head, the spent days of our youth now hitting me true, truer than ever before. The sudden chirp of my cell phone brought me back to reality. The Duke Blue Devils basketball game had ended. Dan, ready for a beer, wanted to get picked up.

By the time we reached the Blue Branch again, Benjie and his girlfriend, Lauren, were busy in the kitchen helping with supper preparations. Hugs and introductions followed, with frozen Margaritas, beer, and a toast. I could almost hear wedding bells in their not-too-distant future. The only thing missing was Kerry.

It had been a long time, too long since our last trip, and the first time I hadn't contributed something to the meal. I enjoyed watching Taylor as he sliced a loaf of French bread lengthwise, applying a mixture of mozzarella cheese, Parmesan, mayonnaise, and chopped olives before shoving it into the oven. I watched Benjie-the-architect sauté a pan of green beans, quiet and reserved, his face a composite of all the handsome aspects of his father and grandfather, magnified about a hundred times. He'd be turning thirty-nine in a few short hours, a confirmed bachelor if he doesn't marry soon. They were just little tykes when Dan and I moved away. And with the day so rushed I hadn't bought a thing for his birthday, but perhaps just being together was enough.

After supper we walked outside to take in the stars, not as brilliant as in years past when the night sky was a cyberstorm of stars. Light pollution has all but erased the Milky Way, but we made the best of it after Benjie set up his telescope, Dan pointing out the four moons surrounding Jupiter as we took turns viewing them before retiring for the evening.

On Sunday morning, our last full day at the ranch, we visited over coffee in the living room, Taylor busy grading papers on the rump-sprung sofa, no lofty conversation forthcoming so early in the day. I noticed Dad's old tool collection hanging in an unorganized knot behind the wood stove as Dan bragged about his instant coffee from Starbucks, Benjie giving him a skeptical look until Dan handed him the rest of his VIA package, wishing him a "Happy Birthday" to laughter all around.

With the boys leaving at noon or after, we took some group pictures around the new chicken coop. When I told them how nice the cabin looked, I could see the relief in their faces, hugging them goodbye before setting off for a drive through the back country, our destination the San Marcos River and the campground where we were married thirty years before, taking in the fields of wildflowers along the way.

We stopped by the ranch Monday morning before heading out. We'd squeezed every ounce of joy we could muster during our long weekend, but it was time to get back to our tropical plant business in Raleigh. We visited with Ben at the dining table as he sorted through a pile of seed packets, handing me a small jar of honey on our way out. As I waved goodbye from the car, I glanced back at the cabin. When I left thirty years ago, I assumed nothing would ever change, everything and everybody would remain frozen in time. But with death comes rebirth and renewal. In my mind, my grandparents will forever be waltzing across their beloved state of Texas. And Mother will be sitting on the porch of the cabin smoking a Kent. Daddy's footprints will always be there, along with so many others who passed before him. Never gone, just out of sight. ❧

THE END

Left to right: Taylor, the author, Ben and brother Ben, 2016

Epilogue

Coda

When I think of bygone days
I think how evening follows morn;
So many I loved were not yet dead,
So many I love were not yet born

— THE MIDDLE BY OGDEN NASH

After the pandemic leveled off in the spring of 2022, we were ready to travel, ready to get back to Texas. It had been a long and harsh two years of isolation for us, beginning with my husband Dan's hospitalization for COVID-19 in the winter of 2020 that put him in ICU and, briefly, on a ventilator. When I saw my husband on that ventilator, I felt like I'd been shaken from the magnolias. Thinking I might lose him was the worst feeling in the world. Aside from the wonderful nursing staff, the one person who got me through my ordeal was Dan's sister, Shelby, an RN at Rex Hospital in Raleigh. Though she wasn't familiar with the new regional hospital Dan was in, she already knew some of the doctors and met with the nursing staff, putting my mind at ease that first day. The hospital was on lockdown, meaning the cafeteria had been shelved, and

187

the family waiting areas roped off. All access doors had been locked with one entry at the ER where visitors had to check in, get a wristband and a temperature check. Masks were mandatory. Shelby was the only person authorized to visit her brother besides me, and only one person at a time was allowed in his room. I kept up with family members by text messages and Kerry called me every night for a report.

We spent Christmas together in the hospital and, thankfully, Dan was discharged the week before New Year's Eve, a bit shaky, but on the mend. Even so, life as we'd known it had changed drastically. No more workouts at the local gym. No more movie matinees. No dining out. No book club meetings. Church services, weddings, and funerals had been cancelled along with dental appointments. Goodbye to all the concerts and street festivals we'd planned to attend, along with March Madness. With our social calendar as clean as new-fallen snow, we watched the national news each evening in horror as the death count kept on climbing. When the vaccine finally came out, we rushed to another town to get it.

After we decided to make the trip, there were so few options for air travel that we decided to drive, leaving our farm in the Carolinas the first week of March. We hadn't seen my family for five years, not since my nephew Benjie's wedding to Lauren in March of 2017. Scarcely a year after their wedding, Ben and Lauren announced they were expecting a new member of the Perry family. And faster than you could say "Daddy's gone to get a rabbit skin to wrap the baby bunting in," in 2019 they had a beautiful baby boy, Jackson, born on my father's birthday, August 12.

We'd meant to get back to Texas sooner, but in the summer of 2019, we were deeply involved in the process of selling our tropical plant business so we could retire. Time simply got away from us as time tends to do. Then COVID blew in like the breath of Satan, and all our travel plans went right out the window.

For a couple of retirees, the long drive to Texas proved tedious at best. Not the easy glide it had been in our thirties when we couldn't afford to fly. There were more eighteen-wheelers to navigate than ever before. Add to that the constant road construction throughout many states, the Kamikaze drivers getting through Atlanta, the gridlock outside of Mobile, and the traffic jams once we reached the outskirts of Houston, and you have full-blown exhaustion.

We decompressed for a couple of days with my ex-sister-in-law, Cathy, and her husband, Steve, at their house in West University Place, my old neighborhood. West University Place is the town that raised me, the little city within the city of Houston that began as a working-class community of modest homes financed on the GI Bill. Except for the street signs, there's little sense of the *place* these days. In my absence, the area has undergone a radical facelift; most of the old cottages and bungalows of my youth have been demolished to make way for McMansions. I grew up on Riley Street a few blocks away from Cathy, where my family's white stucco house has been replaced by a two-story showcase home straight out of *Architectural Digest*. Despite all the changes, I still love the neighborhood. But in reality, we'd be hard-pressed to afford a house or even a lot nowadays. And with all the moneyed people moving in, crime has escalated. Steve said cameras have been set up at all the main arteries to monitor all the cars as they come and go.

Cathy and Steve remodeled their house without taking away from its original character and charm, adding a half-story with two bedrooms upstairs and bumping out the back for a master bedroom and bath, yet leaving the gray façade in front as undisturbed and pristine as the day the little cottage was built back in the 1940s. During the remodeling, Cathy, in typical fashion, named the house Lily the Gray Ghost. She said Lily had been neglected and had fallen into disrepair, that they were helping her shed her old skin. Although it would be considered a teardown these days, they're sitting on a gold mine.

During our stay, we managed to eat at some of the places on our bucket list. Cathy and Steve treated us to a leisurely supper at the Briar Club. The next day, we met cousins Pam and Lauran for lunch at Irma's Original Mexican Experience in downtown Houston. I felt like a country mouse come to the city with all the skyscrapers towering over us as we parked. Once inside, the atmosphere felt like a cozy Spanish village, my chile rellenos entre everything I'd hoped for, the tres leches cake a pleasant surprise. It was so great to spend time with my cousins again after such a long drought.

On our second day at Lily the Gray Ghost, my nephew Ben dropped by with Jackson. I was elated to finally meet my grand-nephew, three years old and cute as a bug. As we hugged, Benjie told me that he and Lauren are expecting another boy in May. Bingo!

On Friday, our third day, we lunched with Cathy and Steve at Blood Brothers BBQ. The line was out the door when we arrived at eleven o'clock, the patrons inside taking pictures of their plates to post on social media as we studied the menu. After lunching on brisket and ribs, we said our goodbyes in the parking lot.

We'd been cautioned to get out of town early to beat the traffic. When we finally maneuvered through the back streets of west Houston and out to the Katy freeway, I hardly recognized any of the old landmarks along the way. I craned my neck a couple of times to see if the Mason Jar or Las Alamedas, two eateries we once frequented, were still around. In the last couple of years, the Katy freeway, or Interstate 10 West, has gone through a metamorphosis. Factoring in the HOV lanes, I counted twelve lanes across with more toll roads and overpasses than I remembered. At its widest, the Katy freeway is twenty-six lanes across. "Heaven help us if we make a wrong turn and end up on the Grand Parkway. We'll be halfway to Beaumont before we can turn around," I said facetiously. The Grand Parkway is now the biggest loop in America. And while I know it helps commuters in outlying towns, I can only think of it as the hamster wheel from hell.

Once we left the Houston city limits, the sea of concrete narrowed down to four lanes and I noticed a sign advertising the Cinco Ranch, an enormous housing development near Katy, a town that was once just a bump in the road. We were twenty miles past Katy before the development subsided and the rice fields called the Katy Prairie appeared. I read in the local paper that a Katy-based developer has purchased a parcel of land in Round Top, a small town east of La Grange, population 90, where a luxury community of "ranchettes" is in the making.

I breathed a sigh of relief when we finally took the Austin bypass and headed for the Blue Branch on Texas 71, where everything looked familiar again. The black Angus cattle dotting the landscape reminded me of big black gumdrops, the open country relaxing. I kept my eyes peeled for the bluebonnets I hoped to see, but only spotted one small patch in the median as we sped by. During our trip five years ago, the roadsides and pastures were a blanket of blue. Bluebonnets can be fickle but it's been a dry spring in the Hill Country.

Twenty minutes later, we took the exit to the ranch and bumped across the cattle guard. I couldn't take my eyes off of the Perry Oak in all its grandeur as we passed the big house to park. My heart skipped a few beats when I spotted Kerry raking weeds from the back of the cabin. Dressed in shorts and a ball cap, he was busy, as usual. I jumped out of the minivan and gave him a big hug and a peck on the cheek. We hadn't seen him in three long years.

As we visited outside, Kerry said he'd stopped at Enchanted Rock to do some rock climbing on his way from Denver. Enchanted Rock is a massive granite dome and state natural area in the Hill Country north of Fredericksburg. My brother used to go rock climbing there in his youth, and we camped there as a family decades ago.

"I was making my way up the rock face when I came to this fissure," he said. "And there was a canyon wren inside the crack right in front of my face, balancing with his claws to either side, hopping up and up in search of bugs," he said in the animated way he has when telling a story, using his hands to mimic the wren's claws against the rock. He looked happy and healthy and I savored every moment of his story.

He went on to explain that he was trying to fix a plumbing leak in the cabin. A pipe had burst beneath it during a bad freeze and my brother, experiencing chronic back pain from a wreck months before, didn't feel up to the task. Kerry said that after he removed some of the siding to dig a trench for access to the water pipes, he discovered termite damage that also needed to be addressed. He'd already torn out the damaged wood and needed to make a trip to the lumber yard.

We followed him to the porch and found quite a mess. The cabin looked like it has been turned upside down and shaken. After such a long hiatus, I didn't expect perfection. Neither did I expect to find a queen mattress that took up much of the porch space. Add to that the big holes in the sofa where a family of mice had had a field day with the stuffing, and the lounging we're accustomed to would be out for the weekend. Kerry said the mattress belonged to my nephew Benjie. He and Taylor are in the process of adding two new bedrooms to the ranch house, a project that's almost finished.

After Kerry left, we walked to the big house to visit with Ben, who looked weak as pond water as he sat in his recliner. There are always things that need fixing at the ranch and I'm sure he was feeling frustrated, so when I saw Kerry pull back in, I left Dan with my brother and joined Kerry.

Since Kerry planned to sleep in the cabin, he was determined to get the plumbing fixed first. I hated the thought of him getting under the cabin, but he reassured me he didn't have to go too far and led me to the other end where he'd dug out a trench under the bathroom. I stood and watched as he spread out a tarp, laid down on his back, and switched on his headlamp, grinning at me as he slid under. I handed him tools as he called for them and before long, he slid back out, smiling as he gave me a thumb's up. Busy hands, happy heart.

After gathering his tools, Kerry said he needed to wait for the plumber's cement to cure for a while before he ran any water, so we hiked down to the swimming hole, dodging fire ant mounds along the way. I could tell rain had been scarce by the ratty brown weeds at the pond. Even the cattails looked parched. The creek was running low and slow and there were piles of tree limbs and detritus high up on the banks that spoke of a flood sometime during the past year.

Kerry stood above the blue hole and posed for a picture, looking snappy in his orange ball cap, Carhartt pants, and hiking boots. The water looked fresh and clean, but I was more interested in locating the rocky outcrop where my grandparents had carved their initials back in 1916. I thought I knew exactly where it was, but tall weeds had taken over the area, and I kept my eyes peeled for snakes. When I thought I'd located the right place, it seemed different somehow. That's when Kerry said a flood must have carried the overhanging rock away, pointing to a large chunk below us, sitting in the creek.

"Maybe we could manhandle it out somehow, or get a tractor," he said, trying to be helpful and supportive while my heart was sinking by the minute.

How can this be? It's been there over a hundred years. How can it be gone? I was crestfallen, to say the least. No way to put it back. I thought about the power of water. Texas floods can be wicked. I remember a flash flood on the San Marcos River that lifted a school bus and carried it downstream. And that time the Blanco River flooded, tearing a house off of its concrete piers and sweeping it through a low water bridge. None of the occupants survived.

We expected my nephews and their wives sometime in the late afternoon. The plan was that we'd eat supper together at Las Fuentes, one of two Tex-Mex places in town. But as the evening progressed, I got a text from young Ben stating they'd wait and come on Saturday. Then, as suppertime drew near, Taylor sent a text stating he and Annie were running late. By then, the wind had gone out of brother Ben's sails, so Dan, Kerry, and I drove into town and ate more barbecue at the Back Porch. The waitress brought us a generous basket of fried pickle chips that we gobbled up until she brought out three barbecue plates. Kerry attacked his brisket like he hadn't eaten in weeks. Why is it so satisfying watching your child eat? Perhaps it's something primal but it's one of the things I miss. It's always the little things, isn't it?

After a light breakfast at our hotel on Saturday morning, Dan and I drove to Weikcl's Bakery down the street and picked up a package of cheese kolaches to take to the cabin. On the way there, we stopped at City Cemetery so I could put some fresh silk flowers on my parents' graves. Before we left the Carolinas, I bought some lovely long-stemmed yellow roses, Mother's favorite, amazed at what the harsh Texas sun had done to the bouquet of silk flowers I'd put there five years ago. As I pulled the ratty arrangement of barren stems from the heavy concrete vase, Dan dumped out the rocks we'd gathered ages ago for ballast to keep the wind from blowing the flowers to Kingdom Come. A healthy bluebonnet plant that managed to thrive at the base of my mother's headstone gave me pause. In another month it would be full of blooms, just in time for Mom's birthday.

The ones who love us best are the ones we'll lay to rest, I thought to myself as we turned to leave. On our way to the car, I mentioned that I'm the only one who replaces the flowers. Dan said he hasn't been good about visiting his parents' graves over the years. When I was a girl, I used to follow my grandparents around from stone to stone as they spruced up my great-grandparents' graves, along with those of Granddad's two brothers, Kurt and Roy, who'd died so tragically early in life. It was obvious from driving the grounds, that many others keep up with this practice. Still, I like the way the people of Mexico celebrate their dearly departed with a day that begins the first of November of each year. They call it *Dia de los Muertos*, Day of the Dead, and gather for picnics at the cemetery where families lay all manner of fresh flowers, framed pictures of loved ones and favorite foods of the deceased. The southern states held Decoration Days after the Civil War, and Memorial Day honors all those who served to protect our freedom. There was a stick flag on Daddy's grave last time I visited. But I think the people of Mexico have the right idea.

My nephew Taylor was busy helping Kerry with cabin repairs when we arrived at the Blue Branch. He stopped long enough to give me a big hug and we exchanged pleasantries before he returned to the task at hand. "Annie's in the big house visiting with Dad," he said over his shoulder as Dan inspected their progress and I carried the kolaches into the cabin.

I decided to go on to the house and pulled out a box of assorted memorabilia I'd brought for Ben from the minivan, joining him as he and Annie visited at the dining table. Annie brought me up to date on married life, and when the conversation paused, I handed Ben a small box containing Dad's old Bulova wrist watch, his high school ring dated 1937, and some military pins that included a sharpshooter medal. After Ben said he'd put them in the gun safe, I handed him a copy of the *Texas Magazine* from 1974, featuring his picture on the cover of a photo essay about a rock-climbing excursion at Enchanted Rock that included our cousin Mark and two of their friends. He seemed happy to get it and I was glad to put a few things I'd stashed away through the years into the right hands.

Annie had to get back to Houston, and after her car pulled away, I carried a chair from the cabin and watched Kerry and Taylor in action, joking and laughing as they took turns sawing two-by-fours and sheets of plywood to cover the area where the lap siding had been. We'd been lucky with the weather which continued to be sunny and mild. That evening, Dan and I treated Ben, Taylor, and Kerry to supper at the old Guadalajara restaurant, the other Tex-Mex place in town that has changed ownership since our last visit. Now Alejandra's, the place looked the same inside, festive and hopping with patrons. While we studied the menu, Ben ordered a beer, the rest of us frozen margaritas that came in big frosty goblets.

I guess the goblet of tequila went right to my head because I don't remember a snippet of our conversation that evening. I do recall the laughter, and the moment when Taylor leaned across the table, excited to tell me that he and Annie were going to start a family. Wonderful news!

We checked out of the hotel on Sunday morning and visited with Ben in the dooryard, sitting beneath the pecan tree while Kerry and Taylor made roof repairs to the old kitchen. We bid our goodbyes in early afternoon, our plans already set to visit Fritzeen and her husband in Kerrville, a three-hour drive from La Grange. They'd sold their home out in California after retirement, making the move right before the pandemic officially grounded everybody. It had been eighteen years since I'd seen Fritzeen, and Kay and her husband planned to join us for our long-awaited reunion.

I had mixed emotions about leaving, but all the local hotels were booked solid for a cowboy festival at the fairgrounds, and the B&B on the main drag in town, Brendon Manor, had been sold and shuttered, another victim of the pandemic, I suppose. Not to mention Prause's Market sitting dark and deserted on the town square. No more hot links forevermore. Before we left, I tossed the plastic golf club set I'd brought for little Jackson onto his bed, and, in parting, Taylor, bless his heart, assured me the new bedroom additions would be completed and we'd have a place to stay next trip.

As we passed beneath the Perry Oak on our way out, I thought about my grandparents' initials sitting at the bottom of the creek, wondering what the future holds for the Blue Branch. Will it remain in the family for another hundred years? Or get turned into an upscale housing community with pickleball courts everywhere? Or, heaven forbid, end up buried under an ocean of concrete. Will the grand old oak be around for future generations to enjoy?

I try not to dwell on it.

Dad's 90th birthday gathering, 2010

Author's Note

If you grew up in Texas, you know that Texas is always in your blood. No matter how far you may travel, the eyes of Texas are upon you, all the livelong day. After thirty-plus years of marriage, Dan still likes to tell people that he had to sneak me across the state line in the dark of night. The truth is, I'm still tethered there.

The first time my parents visited us in North Carolina, Dad kept asking the same question: "Where are all the fences?" And I couldn't help but smile the night he phoned Granddad to check in and made the comment, "It looks a lot like East Texas."

One of the truisms of life is that you spend the first half of it looking forward and the last half looking back, reflecting on the past. Sometimes the picture is blurry, other times sharp as a tack. Though I didn't know it at the time, this memoir began to take shape with the first essay I wrote for the *Houston Chronicle* in the spring of 2000: "Blue Hole, a timeless touchstone." Not long after that, I began keeping a journal both during and immediately after I returned from my trips to Texas and the Blue Branch. I didn't really know where it was going, but I kept at it. Though some of my essays embrace happy times, through journaling I was able to work through some tumultuous times as well.

In her book, *Handling the Truth: On the Writing of Memoir*, Beth Kephart states that "no memoir is worth reading if it is not leavened with beauty and love. And no memoirist should start her work until she can, with authority, write about the things she loves." And I certainly feel that I have done that. When all is said and done, the Blue Branch has always been my happy place.

A memoir has to be truthful, but not necessarily accurate. This sounds like an oxymoron but it's a tidbit of advice I picked up at one of the writer's conferences I attended over the years, advice I've tried my best to follow. I've always been a journalist at heart and tried to write with empathy. After I decided to publish, I sent various chapters to the people who appear within these pages, hoping for true assessments, and in the case of retold stories, for accuracy. Even so, sometimes life and art can conspire against you. I hope this isn't the case here. In the final analysis, this is my story, this is my song. And I hope you enjoy it.